I0866512

# PRACTICAL GUNDOG TRAINING

Nick Ridley and Fran Ardley

# PRACTICAL GUNDOG TRAINING

Nick Ridley and Fran Ardley

Quiller

Copyright © 2025 Nick Ridley and Fran Ardley

Images © 2025 Nick Ridley

First published in the UK in 2025 by Quiller,
an imprint of Amberley Publishing

British Library Cataloguing-in-Publication Data
A catalogue record for this book is available from the British Library.

Paperback ISBN 978 1 84689 408 4
E-book ISBN 978 1 84689 409 1

The right of Nick Ridley and Fran Ardley to be identified as the authors of this work has been asserted in accordance with the Copyright, Design and Patent Act 1988.

The information in this book is true and complete to the best of our knowledge. All recommendations are made without any guarantee on the part of the Publisher, who also disclaims any liability incurred in connection with the use of this data or specific details.

All rights reserved. No part of this book may be reproduced or transmitted in any form or by any means, electronic or mechanical including photocopying, recording or by any information storage and retrieval system, without permission from the Publisher in writing.

Photographs by Nick Ridley
Book design by Becky Bowyer

Appointed GPSR EU Representative: Easy Access System Europe Oü, 16879218
Address: Mustamäe tee 50, 10621, Tallinn, Estonia
Contact Details: gpsr.requests@easproject.com, +358 40 500 3575

**Quiller**
**An imprint of Amberley Publishing Ltd**
The Hill, Merrywalks, Stroud GL5 4EP
Tel: 01453 847800
Email: info@quillerbooks.com
Website: www.quillerpublishing.com
Printed in China

# Contents


Foreword by Jenny Campbell 7
Introduction 9
1. Should You Walk Your Gundog? 13
2. The Place Board 17
3. Place Board Progression 29
4. Retrieving 41
5. Heelwork 69
6. Marking 75
7. Hunting 83
8. Introducing Whistle Commands 97
9. Steadiness 111
10. Introduction to Shot 129
11. Gun Sense 135
12. Introducing Cold Game 141
13. Obstacles 147
14. Scent and Lines 157
15. Working With Another Dog 167
16. Directions 175
17. Water Work 183
18. Picking Up 191
19. Beating 199
20. Shooting Over Your Dog 209
21. Managing Your Dog on a Shoot Day 217
22. Gundog Terminology 225
Acknowledgements 235
Index 237

# Foreword

## *by Jenny Campbell*

This is a refreshing new gundog training book, aimed at all levels of experience. I like the number of exercises that are shared. I can see myself picking up the book and looking for an exercise I want to do with my dogs today. As well as, of course, getting the fundamentals in place at the beginning. A must for every gundog enthusiast!

Former Dragon/investor on the BBC's *Dragons' Den*. In 2020 Jenny Campbell was elected as a Board Director of The Kennel Club. Jenny stood down from the board in 2022 as directorship prohibited her from exhibiting at Crufts, the world's greatest dog show, which she was not prepared to give up (for now). She remains closely connected to The Kennel Club and actively engaged on a number of committees and working groups. Jenny shows, judges, and works her chosen gundogs, the flat-coated retriever www.ronevorg.com

# Introduction

Dogs were first used in the shooting field in the late seventeenth century when shooting birds on the wing became more common. By the late 1700s the term 'gundog' was commonplace. The dogs being used were mainly pointers and setters, in addition to what were commonly known as 'waterdogs', used for duck and goose shooting. As the sport developed, so did the breed types. 'Land spaniels' and specific retrieving breeds such as the Labrador retriever came to be used.

As well as the gundogs developing over the years, so have training practices and techniques. Back in the day the term 'breaking' was often used in both horse and gundog training. Some of the methods used are, quite rightly, not acceptable today. It should not be forgotten that gundogs have been selectively bred to work in the shooting field, and consequently many are high drive and need plenty of mental stimulation. In truth Fran and I don't walk our dogs, but they get plenty of mental and physical exercise through working in the field and, of course, their daily training routine. We hope this is where owners of any gundog breed will find this book a useful aid.

Letting a gundog have free rein to hunt and 'self-reward' is asking for trouble. There is a saying that a gundog views the big wide world as a child would a toy shop. There are loads of exciting things to do and those toys are far more exciting than the parents. Those who have children will have seen, or personally experienced, the embarrassment of trying to get a highly charged child out of a toy shop. Once a young gundog has experienced the excitement and thrill of free-hunting a hedge line and the chase of a blackbird that it has flushed, the owner will have a real challenge on their hands. If you only take one piece of advice from the pages of this book it should be to work hard to make yourself the most important thing in that dog's world. This can be achieved through being consistent in your training.

Never let the dog second-guess you and do not be in too much of a hurry to move on. A house is built on solid foundations and that is the same with gundog training. No matter what you hope to achieve with your dog, you need to have the basics in place. Never be afraid to go back a step or two with your training; and remember there will be highs and lows. Gundog training is like riding on a roller-coaster. One minute you will be at the top and all your training will go to plan and the next minute you are at the bottom, deflated and frustrated. You will often be left wondering if you have been wasting your time. We have all been there and the important thing is to realise that these dogs are not robots and, like us, they will have good and bad days.

If things are not going to plan, put the dog away and start anew tomorrow. Don't compare your dog with others. Social media can have a demoralising effect on a novice trainer as it can appear that the 'film star' dogs never go wrong, they hunt like demons, retrieve, and deliver to hand perfectly. Remember, there are few gundog trainers that are willing to share and show their mistakes. The reality is that no dog is perfect 100 per cent of the time; if they were, this whole gundog training business would be a cinch.

So, how will you manage to train the gundog of your dreams? First of all, it will help to have a goal as to what you eventually want to do with your gundog. Do you want a peg dog? A beating dog? A picking-up dog? Or a dog that you can shoot over? In truth, most of us want all the above and that's what we call a 'versatile gundog'. This is where this book will give you some guidance.

You will also need to follow the three P's: perseverance, persistence and, most importantly, patience. There will be times when you will want to give it all up and you will have to dig deep and persevere, even if that means coming back to a particular exercise another day. There will be times when your dog just keeps pushing the boundaries and you may have to persist in a particular exercise until you and the dog get it right. There will be times when your dog will push you to the limits of your self-restraint, but this is where the most important 'P' comes into effect. Patience is something you will need in bucketloads. Never, ever lose your temper with your dog, no matter how frustrated you get. Take a deep breath and, if need be, put the dog back in the car and try to work out what is going wrong. It could be a combination of both you and the dog so having a break is a good way of resetting the situation. Remember, tomorrow is a new day.

Training a gundog is an investment in many ways. It can be a financial one, especially if you seek the help of a competent and knowledgeable trainer. One that not only understands the work of a gundog, but also one that has practical experience of working gundogs in the shooting field. It is certainly an investment in time and effort. It can easily take anything up to two years before your dog is ready to take into the shooting field and with luck you could have your shooting companion by your side for another ten years, so don't rush your training. Make sure that each element of your training is fully embedded and understood by the dog before moving on to the next phase.

*Practical Gundog Training* takes a different approach to many other gundog training books and does not concentrate on the breed, but rather exercises that owners of all gundog breeds can follow. The training exercises and methods are based on more than fifty years of combined practical experiences of working gundogs in the shooting field. The aim of this book is to offer a simple, straightforward, and easy-to-follow guide. There are no gimmicks, just sound practical advice that will help both novice and the more experienced trainer to get the most out of their gundog.

The book covers specific training and shooting scenarios including place board training, whistle work and working with more than one dog. Each chapter will go through various exercise options and will not only cover the initial training of the subject but also offer ways to introduce some refresher training, which is especially important at the end of a busy working season. Try to keep your training fun for the dog. Too many handlers take the drive and desire out of their dogs by being too strict and imposing obedience too soon. Remember your gundog is a still a dog and needs some time out. Ten minutes' training a couple of times a day is better than hour upon hour. Quite often giving the dog a week or so off from training can not only refresh the dog, but also the trainer as well. Training should be a pleasure not a chore.

Two final pieces of advice. Many novice trainers tend to repeatedly do exercises they know their dogs can do and avoid training exercises that the dogs (or the handlers) find testing. You should always try to avoid setting the dog up to fail, but equally you should be prepared to test both yourself and the dog. Secondly, as trainers we quite often focus on the negative things that have happened during a training session and forget the positive aspects. If you are having a challenging session, try and finish on a high by doing a simple task so that you end on a positive note.

We hope that you find *Practical Gundog Training* both useful and inspirational. It has been a pleasure to share our experience with you and we look forward to meeting you and your dogs at some point in the shooting field.

**Nick Ridley**
**Pettycord Gundogs**

**Fran Ardley, Tarncrag Gundogs**

# 1. Should You Walk Your Gundog?

Whether to walk or not to walk your gundog may seem a strange opening chapter for a training book but how, when and where you exercise your gundog will have an effect on the dog's ongoing training regime. It has already been mentioned that it is imperative that your dog sees you as the centre of its world. Everything good has to come from you and that will ultimately give you a level of control over what you must never forget is a highly driven canine hunting machine. A gundog not only needs physical stimulation but more importantly it needs mental stimulation, and you can achieve both by using focused exercise. If you walk your dog 5 miles a day all you are doing is making it fitter and, of course, a hard-working gundog has to be fit, but ten or fifteen minutes of the correct kind of exercise will not only work the dog's body but also it will have to use its mental capacity as well and that will help tire the dog out.

The biggest problem with 'just walking the dog' is that the chances are you as the handler will not be concentrating on the dog and it will take full advantage of your lack of attention. Dogs are great opportunists and while you are engrossed in conversation with your walking partner or scanning the latest gundog training advice on social media, your dog will have one eye on you and another on the local squirrel population and there will only be one winner – and it won't be you! Whilst out on a 'walk' many owners will be constantly nagging at the dog to come back to them with little or no reward and eventually the dog will get bored with the constant white noise and ignore the command. Engaging with your gundog whenever you are outside should be a priority. If you feel you do need to take your dog out for a walk try to vary your route: that way the dog won't pre-empt where they are heading. Keep changing direction, perhaps don't even have a destination in mind – if you keep the dog guessing you will keep it focused.

Many of the exercises in this book can be incorporated into the dog's daily exercise routine. For example, memory retrieves are a great way of doing a bit of training and giving your dog both mental and controlled physical exercise. If time is short this is a way of getting the dog to do double the amount of running that it would do if it just wandered along with the handler; also it gives the dog something to focus on and stimulates it mentally at the same time. Imagine you have a bubble of around 25 metres around you and when the dog is not engaged in doing a retrieve or some other controlled exercise it needs to stay within that bubble. Consider it your safety net: if the dog is within that space the chances are you will be able to pre-empt and prevent any chance of it getting distracted and running off. That is, of course, providing you are paying attention to the dog and not getting distracted with the many other aspects of daily life.

... if you keep the dog guessing you will keep it focused.

# 2. The Place Board

No matter what your eventual hopes are for you and your gundog, the one thing that you will need to build is the solid foundations of the basics. Your dog will need to sit on command, whether that is a verbal command, a whistle command, a hand signal, or a combination. He will need to stay on a given spot until given a further instruction and he will need to recall both verbally and with a whistle command.

There is a lot of hanging around in the shooting field. Whether your dog is sitting next to you at a peg or waiting in the beating line for the Guns to arrive or sitting way back in a wood waiting to pick up shot game, your gundog must be taught to be patient and sit quietly. The place board is a fairly recent technique to be used in the UK, although in the USA it has been used to train gundogs for many years. Some trainers still think it is a gimmick and wouldn't give it the time of day; however there are plenty of us that have embraced this method and have found that is has really advanced the way we train our gundogs.

There are a few variations of the place board, including hula hoops and, more recently, a square that is made from tape and pegged out on the grass, called an obedience box. From experience, the small step up onto a place board seems to have a psychological effect on the dogs and, as it separates the training area from the ground, it seems to work better.

There is no such a thing as a standard place board. Some trainers use home-made boards and others use purpose-made boards, such as the Cato place board. Ideally, they need to be a rectangular shape because this helps to guide the dog, like a runway, during the training exercises. The dimensions of the board should be around 40 cm (wide) x 60 cm (long) and around 9 cm (high) and ideally covered with a non-slip surface such as artificial turf, or a rubber mat. It should be sturdy enough not to move should an enthusiastic dog jump on it. One benefit is that it gives the dog a 'target' area and also, the trainer knows exactly where they are positioning the dog. Without doubt, the biggest advantage is that you can use the technique in the back garden or even indoors and therefore you can start basic training from quite an early age. It gives a level of consistency to a young pup's early training and in the longer term it can help to prevent some of the common problems such as creeping forward or poor delivery of retrieves.

**... your gundog must be taught to be patient and sit quietly.**

You can begin your place board training with your pup as soon as it has settled into its new home, and it never fails to amaze how quickly they gasp the concept. The aim is to make the board a good place for the pup to be: only good things happen when they are on the place board. That may be a gentle chest stroke or a small treat. Giving treats in gundog training is a contentious issue and one that causes plenty of discussion. If overdone

The Cato place board is a purpose-built unit that is sturdy and is covered with a non-slip top which is ideal for dogs of all ages and weights.

the dog quickly sees the trainer and their hands simply as a vending machine that is constantly dishing out tasty morsels. Reward and praise don't always have to come in the form of food: they can also be both verbal and physical. That said, when conditioning a pup to the place board the reward of a small treat can really speed up the process.

As already mentioned, you can introduce the place board to pups from quite a young age but remember this is not training it is conditioning and any training sessions should be kept short. You will need an area that has no distractions: you can use your patio, garage, or back garden, but you want somewhere that is distraction free. Get yourself prepared before any training session. Get the board set up and have a few high-value treats put away in your pocket. The trainer's positioning in front of the board is very important. Always stand at the end of the place board, as if you were to 'walk the plank', as this will help to encourage the pup to eventually use the board like a short runway, which will really pay dividends when moving on to retrieving exercises.

Although you can begin the process with the pup loose it is easier with it on a lead. Encourage the dog up onto the board, saying the word 'place'. Use a very small treat to lure the pup onto the place board. You may find that initially the pup is reluctant to climb onto the board but be patient and stay calm. Remember, the place board has to be seen as a good place for the pup. Once the pup is on the board tell him to 'sit'. If you have success give him a treat, then ask the pup to leave the board by a little tug on the lead. Walk a small circle back to the board and repeat the commands. You may be surprised how quickly the pup gains confidence and you may be tempted push on but remember to always finish on a good note and never let the pup get bored with the exercise. It is important that you, as the trainer, release the pup from the board, so don't let it get off and wander about when it wants to. This is why it is a good idea to initially use a lead to control the dog.

There is a training method where the dog is 'loaded' with treats when it is on the board. This simply means several food treats are given in quick

When using the place board, it is important that the handler stands at the long end and this will help encourage the dog to use the board like a little runway.

succession to reward the dog. The problem with this technique is that the dog quickly becomes more focused on the 'hand vending machine' rather than the trainer. Use small pieces of treat and only give it to the dog once as it sits; don't keep loading it with food as it will quickly lose its value to the dog.

During the initial conditioning process, you will be using small treats to get the pup really keen on the board, but you will also begin to give physical praise by gently rubbing the pup's chest and underneath its neck. Keep this praise low-key as you don't

You want to undertake your initial place board training somewhere with no distractions, ideally on a path or patio.

Initially put your dog on a lead and lure it onto the place board with a high-value treat using the command 'place'.

want to overexcite the dog. The purpose of this is to encourage the pup to lift its head up and this will transfer later to a high head delivery of a retrieve. You can also use verbal praise but keep it calm and quiet. Gradually, begin to delay the length of time before you reward the dog and mix it up between a treat and a stroke. This will help to teach them that both forms of reward are as important as each other. Eventually you will stop treating with the food. Ideally do no more than ten minutes at a time at this stage. The overall aim is to gradually build up the pup's desire to work on the board to the point that when you go to get it out for a training session the pup is trying to jump on it before you can even get the board on the ground.

Once the pup has accepted sitting on the board, you can then begin to slowly walk around whilst the pup is sitting but is still on the lead. Don't move too far away and if the pup loses eye contact with you, stop until it reconnects eye contact with you again. This is the beginning of getting a good eye contact with the dog which will pay dividends as your training progresses. As you continue you can gently drop the lead on the floor, the pup will still think you have hold of it and this will enable you to begin to gradually move further away. There is a train of thought that once you have given the command 'sit' the dog shouldn't move until given another instruction, but in truth most trainers will use a 'wait' or 'stay' command when they begin to

Place board training can be introduced at quite an early age, and it is surprising how quickly a young pup will learn that the board is a good place to be.

move further away from the dog. It is a matter of choice, but whatever you decide you must be consistent in your instructions; dogs respond better when commands are black and white, do not confuse them by mixing up words. A lot of time in the shooting field is spent hanging around and waiting, so teaching your young dog to sit quietly and do nothing is as important as more exciting aspects of gundog training, but unfortunately it is a skill that too few people take time to teach. It may be boring to both the trainer and the dog, but it is very much a foundation of the dog's training.

Once the pup has accepted the board and understands what you are asking it to do without any confusion and is doing the exercises with enthusiasm, it is time to move the boards to a location where there are more distractions. This could be the local park. Each and every time you begin a new exercise be prepared to go back a few steps and, in this case, by simply moving your training area you may well find your little dog totally forgets what it is supposed to be doing. So, in order to pre-empt this, go back to the beginning and put the lead on and gradually build up the exercise in the new location. If you have done your initial place board training properly the dog will soon regain its focus and be back with you.

Some trainers like to use multiple boards, anything up to four at a time, but in most cases just introducing a second board is sufficient to further the

Eventually the treat can be replaced with physical praise. Stroking the dog under the chest will encourage a high head carriage that will be beneficial later in the dog's training.

Once the dog has accepted the board you can then either drop the lead or remove it altogether and begin to walk around, remembering to maintain eye contact at all times.

By introducing a second place board you can begin to teach the dog a basic recall command and sitting and waiting at a distance.

pup's training. However, this should only be done once the dog has been fully conditioned to the single board. These exercises are the beginning of getting your dog conditioned to sitting and recalling at a distance.

Set your two place boards about a metre apart so you can now ask the pup to go from one board to the other. Initially sit the pup up on one board and at this stage make sure it is back on the lead. Then give the command 'place' and point to the second board and if need be gently lead the dog on to the second board. Because of the previous work you have done with the pup it should sit up and present itself to you. Make sure that the dog is presenting itself every time. This is important because once the dog understands that this is the normal way to place itself when called, it makes a strong foundation for the dog's future delivery of retrieves. Every time you have success remember to reward with a treat, be that food, verbal or physical. If things go well the lead can be discarded, but if at any time it goes wrong, put the lead back on.

Over time you can gradually move the boards further apart and begin to leave the dog sitting on one board whilst you stand behind the second one and call him to you. This is where the shape of the place board comes into play. Remember to use your recall command. This could be 'here' or 'come' and you can precede the command with the dog's name but remember to keep your commands consistent. Don't overdo this exercise as the dog will

Recalling the dog from one place board to another will help ensure that it learns to sit in front of the handler, which is the correct position for the delivery of a retrieve.

quickly pre-empt what is going to happen. Mix it up and quite often walk back to the dog rather than call it to you. Remember, never let the dog second-guess you.

You may find that as you increase the distance between the two boards, when the dog is recalled it gains a bit of speed and may run past you before coming back to the place board. If this happens just position one of the boards in front of a hedge line, or wall, so you can stand between the board and obstacle, and this should solve the problem. A young dog must learn to pace its return and you should find that they quickly remember what they should be doing.

Another thing to watch out for is how long you wait before recalling the dog. A common issue is that the trainer will unconsciously call the dog at about the same length of time and the dog soon works this out and may break the stay or get twitchy at around the time it is expecting to be called. Therefore, it is important to make sure you vary the length of time in between leaving the dog and recalling them.

Positioning the place board in front of a wall or fence will help to prevent the dog running past you if it gains too much speed on a recall.

# 3.
# Place Board Progression

Getting a solid retrieving instinct in a dog that has been bred to hunt is a vital part of its basic training.

If you have been consistent with your place board training, your dog should be fully conditioned to sitting and staying for varying periods on the board and is recalling from one to the other at varying distances. You can now move on to incorporating those learnt behaviours with some basic steadiness, retrieving and delivery exercises.

Getting a strong retrieving instinct in a young gundog is a vitally important part of their training, especially for the hunting breeds such as spaniels, and the hunt, point, retrieve dogs (HPR). These dogs have been selectively bred to hunt and if this is allowed to develop without encouraging the desire to retrieve this will potentially cause real issues, and as you will see later in this book retrieving or the desire to retrieve will ultimately give you a higher degree of control over your dog. The next chapter will deal with retrieving in greater detail.

Now is about the time to introduce some steadiness training. Having a steady gundog in the shooting field is the holy grail. A dog that can sit at a peg or work in the beating line or be off the lead when picking up is worth its weight in gold. But too many gundogs fall short of this, and this is predominantly down to a lack of training. Steadying a dog to a thrown dummy, the fall of a bird, or the flush of a rabbit can be challenging and it can be boring for both the trainer and dog. But it is something that you must work at if you hope to have a dog that you can be proud of. There are many ways of steadying a dog, but the introduction of the place board has made it an easier undertaking. You are building on what the dog has already learnt and understands and you are gradually building the foundations.

If you have done your initial place board training correctly your gundog knows that sitting on the board means that it has to stay there until asked to move, either off or onto another board. To begin this exercise, move the board back onto a solid surface such as a patio, car park, or driveway, basically somewhere there are no distractions. Sit the pup on one board and bounce a tennis ball or drop a dummy in front of you. At this stage you can introduce what can be considered the most important verbal command you will use during the dog's life: 'leave it'. This command will be used throughout the dog's training and into the shooting field. The dog will learn that 'leave it' means just what it says on the tin. Whether it is a dummy, a ball, another dog, a pheasant, or a rabbit the dog is not to retrieve the item, or it is to ignore the distraction. Be consistent with this command and going forward in your training you will quickly realise how useful it is.

**Having a steady gundog in the shooting field is the holy grail.**

Going back to the exercise, if the dog moves off the board put him back on and repeat the process. It may be beneficial to just slip a lead back on the dog. Remember, never be too concerned about taking a step or two back when introducing a new training exercise. Do not allow the dog to pick up the ball or dummy at this stage. Don't just stand in front of the dog whilst you are bouncing the ball or throwing a dummy, walk around the pup as it is sitting on the board and remember to vary your direction and distance from the dog. This will help to keep the dog's focus on you and it adds another steadying element to the exercise.

As this exercise progresses you can introduce more dummies or balls and begin to throw them around the dog. The most tempting one for the dog is a dummy that is thrown over its head. Most dogs will turn to watch

Once your gundog is fully conditioned to the place board you can then begin the process of steadiness and introducing the 'leave it' command.

As you progress through this exercise you can then begin to throw more distraction dummies around the dog including the most tempting, which is one thrown over the dog's head.

the dummy go out and as the dog is now between you and the dummy it is far easier for it to break its position on the board and run in. If the dog does break its stay at any time and picks the retrieve don't make a big fuss, just take it from the dog and set up the exercise again making sure you are in a position to prevent the dog from going wrong again.

Continuing to build on the foundations that you have instilled in your gundog in the previous exercises, you can also use two place boards to build on the steadiness of the dog and also further develop the 'leave it' command. At this stage, your dog should understand the concept of being recalled from one board to another at varying distances and be used to sitting on the board until given a further command. This particular exercise is useful in a practical sense. There may be times in the shooting field when you may need to recall your dog back through a field of shot game and, for whatever reason, you don't want them to retrieve any birds. Having trained the dog to ignore any potential retrieves and recall back to you can help prevent a potentially very embarrassing situation. We have all been there!

Initially sit the dog on the place board and put a dummy to one side of your position at the back of the second board. Recall the dog and be ready to give the command 'leave it'. By beginning the exercise with the distraction retrieve right next to you it helps to give you the opportunity to block the dog should it deviate from coming straight onto the board. However, if you have done your foundation work properly the dog should be totally focused on what you are asking it to do because it has learnt by repetition to come from one board to another.

The ultimate aim of this exercise is to be able to put a number of dummies between the two place boards and recall the dog through them with the 'leave it' command.

The next step is to use the two place board recall exercise but to introduce a distraction dummy.

Gradually move the retrieve nearer the dog's starting point on the first board and don't forget to repeat the 'leave it' command each time before recalling the dog. The aim is to be able to put a number of dummies between you and the dog and for it to ignore them; this will take time and patience but it is a really useful skill to have in your gundog training box.

## The Delivery

Getting a smart delivery from your gundog not only looks good but it also has a very practical purpose. First of all, if your dog makes its retrieve and delivers it back to your hand quickly and without any fuss it makes the whole process far more efficient. Secondly, there is nothing more frustrating than a dog strutting around with a dummy or bird in its mouth and not letting the handler take the retrieve, and this is where the proper use of the place board during the dog's early training will really pay dividends.

Just to recap, by now the dog has been taught to sit and stay on the board until being told it can move off; in fact by now your dog should be desperate to get on the board because it has learnt that it is a good place to be. The dog should fully understand the recall from one board to the next and you have encouraged a 'high head carriage' by praising the dog with a chest and neck rub with your hand. This has also had the added benefit of desensitising the dog to having your hands around its head, so it is less likely to dip its head when you go to take a retrieve.

A downside of constant treat rewarding can be that as you put out your hand to take a retrieve the dog may spit out the dummy as it associates your hand with being given food and that is more valuable than keeping hold of the retrieve. That's one reason why, once the dog understands the action of sitting on the board, you will move to physical reward and praise rather than food treats.

Begin by asking the pup to sit on a board and give the dog a small dummy or ball to hold. It's now that you can introduce the verbal 'hold' command. If the dog does not take the object willingly then give a short-distance retrieve. If you have your foundations in place the dog should come straight back to the board and sit (remember this has been taught and repeated during the initial place board training). Now put yourself at the back of the board just as you have done numerous times before. When the dog is sitting and holding the dummy don't take the retrieve, just go through your normal process of gentle praise by stroking the dog's chest and neck until the dog lifts up its head and then you can take the retrieve with the command 'leave it'.

The next stage is to set the dog up on the board and get it to hold a retrieve. You can then begin to walk around the dog making sure it maintains

The 'hold' command is vital for any gundog that is going to work in the shooting field and this exercise is a progression of all the previous place board lessons.

eye contact with you. If it looks away stop moving until the dog makes eye contact again. In this exercise you are reinforcing not only steadiness, but also the idea to the dog that you may not always take the retrieve from it straight away, and it is to 'hold' until you are ready to take the dummy. Once your dog is happy to sit on the board holding a retrieve for an extended period you can move on to the next stage.

You may be wondering, 'What is the benefit of this exercise?' Imagine you are out either picking up or shooting over your dog. You send it for a retrieve and the dog brings back a runner (pricked bird). You really don't want the dog dumping it at your feet because the bird may well run off and things could get really messy very quickly as the dog tries to catch hold of the fleeing bird. You may not be able to take the retrieve straight away as you may be dealing with another dog in your picking-up team or reloading your gun. If you have taught your gundog to sit and hold on to its retrieve it helps to make the situation far more controllable and efficient.

By now you will be getting the idea that gundog training is a bit like a jigsaw puzzle. You start off with lots of pieces that in the beginning make a fragmented picture and gradually, over time, you and your dog realise that each little piece has its place and will eventually slot into another piece. Before you know it, a picture begins to develop, and it all begins to make sense.

At this point your dog should, sit and stay on the place board, have a nice high head carriage (that has been developed by plenty of gentle physical

You have already taught your dog to sit on the place board whilst you walk around and now you are simply adding the 'hold' into the exercise.

Another progression is to add a second place board and recall the dog whilst it holds a dummy. Using this method you will get a controllable delivery.

praise), be comfortable holding a retrieve whilst sitting on the place board for a varying length of time, and sit still and maintain its hold on a dummy whilst you move around the dog. It is now time to slot in another piece of the puzzle. Remember you can only move on to this exercise if your dog can happily go from one board to the other without a retrieve and also be confident enough to sit on a board with a retrieve in his mouth without spitting it out.

Place a second board about a couple of metres from the first one and with the dog sitting on the first board with the retrieve in its mouth, recall it to the other board. At the same time give the same direction and verbal command as you have always done. Remember your position behind the second board. The dog should confidently go from one board to the other, without dropping the retrieve. Just let the dog sit there for a while and don't take the retrieve from him. Reposition yourself back behind the first board and repeat the exercise. This time you can take the retrieve, and don't forget to praise the dog.

A variation on this exercise is that instead of calling the dog to the second board, you can walk back to the dog and get it to walk to heel with you to the second board whilst carrying the retrieve. Remember never let the dog second-guess what you are going to ask it to do and keep mixing it up; that will help to prevent the dog from getting bored and it will help keep the dog's focus. Obviously, you don't train these exercises just once and think that if you have success that's a job done and it's time to move

Never let the dog second-guess what you are going to do – mix it up. Sometimes go back to the dog and walk it at heel back to the second place board.

on to another task. Dogs learn by repetition, and there is no reason why you shouldn't go back over previous exercises to constantly reinforce the learning process.

A common comment from place board sceptics is why would they want to cart around a place board when they go shooting, beating, or picking up. Of course, the reality is that you don't have to carry a place board with you as your dog will have gone through some transitioning training long before it is ready to go out into the field and that is normally a fairly straightforward process. If you have done your preparation and not rushed your previous training, this should be fairly seamless, but as with all aspects of gundog training that is not always the case.

Initially, take the boards out to your training area. Put one down and then ask the pup to sit on it. Then walk around the pup and once you have the dog's full concentration, throw a retrieve for it, then send the dog. If you get a perfect presentation and delivery do just one more. This time if all goes well take the board away and ask the dog to sit on the ground and repeat the exercise exactly as you did when the dog was on the place board. Throw a retrieve in the same place as before and then ask the dog to fetch it. Hopefully, the dog will go straight out and pick up the retrieve, come back to you and present as it has been conditioned to do when using the board.

If you have done your basic place board training correctly the transition when removing the board should be fairly straightforward.

If everything goes to plan do one more and if you get another successful retrieve and delivery, stop and do no more during that session. You must never be afraid to take a step back should you not get the success you

The place board is a training aid that you will need to revisit during the lifetime of your gundog.

anticipated. If you move on too quickly without the dog fully understanding the lesson, you may develop problems that will become harder to resolve as you progress through your dog's training. Prevention is better than cure.

The use of place boards makes building the foundations of gundog training a far more straightforward process. They can enable the trainer to get the absolute basics in place, whilst they can help a high-drive gundog to settle and focus and they can help to build confidence in a softer-natured dog. Place boards are not a magic wand, but they are a useful tool and something that during your gundog's life you should revisit when it's time for refresher sessions. A well-respected gundog trainer once said that 'a place board is not something you USED to train your gundog, a place board is something you USE to train your gundog'.

# 4. Retrieving

A spaniel has a natural desire to hunt, and this can overcome their desire to retrieve. You need to get the balance right.

All breeds of gundog other than pointers and setters should be expected to retrieve. It is fundamental to their job and a pivotal part of their training. Without a solid retrieving instinct, you may struggle to get the dog to hunt for you: more on that in the next chapter. However, training a gundog to be a dependable retriever can have several pitfalls and all too often we see dogs that are indifferent in their retrieving or have had too much pressure put on them in the formative lessons so that they become reluctant retrievers. Another issue that regularly crops up, mainly in breeds such as spaniels, is that their natural desire to hunt overcomes their desire to retrieve and that can develop into a real problem. In practical terms it's no good having the hardest, flashiest hunting gundog in the world if, when you shoot something, it goes out and ignores the retrieve and carries on hunting. It is a fine balance.

There is a train of thought that if you are just going to use your gundog in the beating line then you may not even want to teach the dog to retrieve, but not many people want to be that restrictive with their dogs. Let's face it, the way you and your dog work in the shooting field may well evolve and so it is better to train for all eventualities. Over the generations gundogs have been selectively bred for natural ability and trainability and, more often than not, any issues that you may come across during the dog's training will be down to environmental influences. Most retrieving issues will come about because of what happens during the non-training time.

It is worth remembering that old adage 'prevention is better than cure'. If you can prevent your gundog from getting into bad retrieving habits, then that is easier than trying to cure bad habits. It is worth noting some of the more common issues that can occur, such as running out and ignoring the retrieve, running off with the retrieve, spitting out or dropping the retrieve, swapping retrieves, poor delivery, running past the handler and a reluctancy to give up a retrieve. There will be plenty of others, but these are certainly the more common problems that can crop up. However, you can put a few basic rules in place to help prevent some of these situations occurring in the first place.

Most gundogs live indoors in a family environment and as a result there will be plenty of opportunities for the dog to run around picking up shoes, remote controls etc., and more often than not they will have a box of toys to keep them amused. If we once again look at the common retrieving problems that can occur, it isn't hard to see how they manifest themselves. You come home and the dog wants to greet you. Most gundogs will be desperate to find something to carry around in their mouths, after all they have been bred for generations to bring game back to their handler. The dog finds your slipper that you left lying around in the hallway, but obviously you

**It is worth remembering that old adage 'prevention is better than cure'.**

don't want dog slobber all over it so you grab it, tell the dog off and so a seed is planted. Unwittingly, you repeat this behaviour over the following few days and, before you know it, you have a dog that is reluctant to bring anything to you or, even worse, as you grab the slipper it decides it doesn't want to give it up and holds on to it. Sound familiar? Going back to our wise old saying 'prevention is better than cure', the prevention is simple: just make sure the dog can't get hold of anything you don't want it to, and you won't develop the issue in the first place.

A current trend in general dog training, and one that has certainly found its way into gundog training, is the constant 'rewarding' of the dog by giving it a treat. There is a time and place for giving a dog a food reward, but when you are training a dog to retrieve is not the time. One of the more common retrieving issues that occur is the dog dropping the dummy as it gets back to the handler, and in most cases that is because it is anticipating the treat reward which it perceives to be of higher value than the retrieve. Remember, the reward for bringing a retrieve back doesn't have to be food. It can be verbal or physical praise.

If you are new to the gundog training world you may well be totally baffled when you look at the numerous and varied designs of retrieving

Most gundogs live in a home environment and it's not unusual to be greeted by your best friends holding your slippers.

dummies on the market. In truth, many of the designs have very little bearing on the dog's actual training and have been designed to train the owner to part with their hard-earned cash. Nevertheless, there is some sound science that as a gundog trainer you can use to your advantage when training your dog to retrieve and the main factors are colour and contrast. The aim of these early retrieving exercises is to get the dog used to fetching an object back to you and to help achieve this we wouldn't normally be hiding dummies in long grass or rough cover. You just want the dog to go out, pick up the dummy and come back so it is better that the odds are stacked in the dog's favour, and the colour of the retrieving item can make a big difference. The question is, what is the optimum colour to use? Well, believe it or not, a blue or purple dummy would seem to be best. If we take a quick look at how and what a dog can see this may make more sense.

The dog has three main aspects to its sight and the first of these is motion. Think of a green lizard, motionless on a leafy branch in the tropics: both you and your dog would have a hard time seeing it, until it moved. Think back to a dog chasing a green tennis ball against green grass, it can follow this fine because it is moving, despite there not being a colour difference on which to 'lock-on'. The second aspect, and this is one that is important to gundog trainers, is contrast (that is something that has an outline against a background). A stationary object that has a very distinct and very different shape from its background is easier to spot, while one that is patterned like its background will blend in. That's the principle of camouflage clothing. Yes, it's the colour of the woods, but more importantly, camo breaks up the

Retrieving dummies are available in a bewildering range of shapes and colours but there is some solid science that can help in your gundog training.

human body's outline against the patchy background scene of branches, leaves, and underbrush. Even small movements are harder to see when an object's outline blurs with its background.

The third is colour and this is equally important. Most people think that dogs see in black and white, but they are in fact 'colour blind'. They see colour but their colour range, or to be scientific, their chromatic acuity is significantly less than humans. This is for two reasons: (1) dogs have fewer cone cells in their retina (cone cells are responsible for seeing colour); and (2) dogs are dichromatic (they see only two primary colours – blue and yellow) whereas humans are trichromatic, meaning we see three primary colours – red, blue, and green.

Consequently, the dog's world consists of yellows, blues, and greys. When a human sees a red object, that same object will look green to the dog and therefore if you thought that by using a red dummy or ball you were helping your dog's confidence when setting out a retrieving exercise, you were in fact making the retrieves harder. The dummy or ball will all but disappear against the backdrop of green vegetation. Evolution is a marvellous thing and way back in time when humans were hunter-gathers, we tended to hunt during the day and we needed to be able to recognise what food was ready to eat. When you think about it the colour of most ripe fruit tends to be towards the red end of the colour spectrum and fruit that is not ready to eat is nearly always green, so our sight patterns evolved so that we were able to see the difference. Wild dogs, however, hunt at dusk and into the night and therefore vivid colour isn't so important but being able to detect movement is critical for survival.

So, to maximise an object's visibility to a dog, we should strive to combine the maximum contrast (a dark and light pattern unlike that of the background scene); and a stand-out colour (one that is identifiable by dogs and does not occur very often in the background scene). The best of

If we understand the science between what colours the human eye can see and what a canine eye can see, we can use this to our advantage when training.

Human eye.

Canine eye.

all possible worlds for most background scenes would therefore be a boldly patterned bright purple/blue and white object. Of course, ultimately, we require our gundogs to use all their natural instincts which include sight, scent, and hearing.

Quite often when starting a young pup's retrieving, we tend to use tennis balls. They leave a good scent trail and are easy for a pup to pick up. But look at the colour spectrum and you will clearly see that green is not a good colour to use especially on grass, as in theory everything would look white to the dog. You can now buy blue tennis balls and they are far better to build the confidence of a pup; the colour will stand out like a beacon and remember at this early stage you want to make it as easy as possible for the puppy. As the dog becomes more experienced and the exercises become more involved, you can again use colour to your advantage and use red balls or dummies which are correspondingly more difficult to see.

As already stated, contrast is also important in a dog's visual arsenal and a black and white dummy thrown out along the ground when a dog is hunting can be very tempting. Rabbits can be the downfall of many of us when hunting our dogs, especially spaniels, and when you think about it, they are the ultimate distraction: they run (movement) and they have a white tail that flashes against a dark body (contrast) and the only thing that evolution missed in making the humble rabbit the ultimate temptation for a dog was that evolution never made them in purple or blue.

Basic retrieving can begin from quite an early age. In fact, the earlier the better but remember two things. Firstly don't overdo it as the dog may get bored, and secondly make it fun for both you and the dog. Too many people try and formalise their retrieving far too early by putting undue pressure on the dog. If you have used the place board method of training, you will also be building up your dog's retrieving desire, but the purpose of this book is not to give the reader just one way of training their dog but to offer various options and ideas. Of course, you can mix and match techniques depending on your ability as a trainer and the temperament of your dog.

An important component of your retrieving training is to be consistent in the command you use to send the dog. It really doesn't matter what word you use but either 'fetch' or 'out' are the most common. Some handlers like to use different commands for seen, memory or blind retrieves, but if you think about it in practical terms that could be quite confusing. Imagine this scenario: you are out shooting over your dog, and it flushes a pheasant from some thick cover (bramble or bracken), the bird gets shot and falls out of sight. Now you have to decide whether the dog saw the bird: a seen retrieve and therefore a corresponding command, or the dog didn't see the bird due to the denseness of the cover and therefore it is a blind retrieve with the corresponding command. If you are consistent with a single-word command

A small light dummy or small tennis ball is an ideal retrieve for a young pup.

during your training, the dog will learn by repetition that when it is given a command using a particular word it simply means there is something for it to find. Just keep it simple.

If you are starting off a young pup, then you will need something small and light for the dog to retrieve and that can be a puppy dummy or a small tennis ball. It really doesn't matter what you use; what's more important is how and where you use it, and there can be a slight difference in whether you have gone down the place board route or not. Ideally, you will need an area to restrict the dog: a hallway, or a passageway down the side of your house is ideal, but if you don't have either of these then you could build a small retrieving lane. This can be simply made up by using some plastic netting supported by plastic fence posts. This is a really quick set up that you can put up in your garden and it can be taken down when not in use. You don't have to make the lane particularly long but don't make it too wide as that can give the dog the opportunity to dive down either side of you. The basic idea is to prevent one of the most common retrieving problems, that of the dog running off with the retrieve.

Either kneel or, even better, sit on the ground and throw out the retrieve. In the initial stages you won't be holding the dog back or preventing it from running out after the ball or dummy. Remember it has to be fun for the dog – all the steadiness can be built in later. You will have already seen that this is a different method from using the place board, but the end result should hopefully be the same. Once the dog has got the retrieve in its mouth

Get down to the dog's level to help encourage it to come back to you with the retrieve. Do not be too quick to take it from the dog. Make it fun.

give it plenty of encouragement and call it back to you. Don't try to make it sit. Let it come into you and if it jumps all over you, so much the better. Give the dog plenty of praise but do not try and take the retrieve straight away. You want the dog to make the connection that bringing something back to you is a good thing. When you are ready you can gently take the ball or dummy and repeat the exercise. Don't overdo this, especially if the dog is young. If you get two or three good results stop and put the retrieve away leaving the dog wanting more, it will be even keener next time. People quite often ask how often they should train their dogs and in truth there are not any hard and fast rules but when they are young two ten-minute sessions a day are far better than an hour session. This will help to keep both you as the trainer and the dog fresh and keen.

As you progress with these basic retrieves you can begin to add a bit more control into the exercise. Sit your dog out in front of you and throw a dummy about halfway between you and him. He will need to be quite steady before you move on to this exercise. Call the dog to you with the command you use to 'fetch' to make the retrieve. Once again at this stage we are limiting how fast the dog can come back to us: as the dog reaches you lift your hands from the waist position and the dog should naturally lift its head thus presenting the dummy. You can introduce the command 'hold' whilst

Setting up a simple retrieve between you and the dog can help to control the dog's excitement.

the dog is sitting in front of you and never rush to take the retrieve; gradually increase the time you let the dog keep hold of the dummy before taking it.

As has already been mentioned, dogs are very perceptive to a handler's body language and quite often a slight shift in the way you stand or move can make a difference to the way the dog reacts. This is especially relevant in the case of getting a good delivery. It is important that you stand upright when your dog is coming in towards you. Many novice handlers will lean in towards the dog and this can have the effect of 'pushing' the dog to one side and as a consequence the handler then tries to make a grab for the dog, and this can lead to the dog becoming reluctant to bring anything back.

Some dogs get into a habit of dropping the retrieve short rather than bringing it all the way and it is not unusual for them to do this at practically the same spot every time. There are two techniques that can be employed to help overcome this and both rely on perfect timing. If the dog is dropping quite close, step into the dog as it is coming in. It is time-critical that the forward movement coincides with the dog reaching the area it normally puts the retrieve down. The step forward is enough to make the dog look up and helps to break the pattern of behaviour so you can then take the dummy. If the dog is dropping further away, employ the exact opposite of the above. As the dog is coming in, step backwards encouraging the dog to come towards

The handler's body position can have a direct effect on the dog. Stand upright when the dog is coming back in with the retrieve.

you. If the dog's recall is sound, this movement will normally be enough to make the dog follow. Over time shorten the distance you walk back until, eventually, the dog is back on track again and delivering to hand.

If you have followed the place board method of training, you should have a developed a solid delivery in your dog. However, if you decided place boards are not for you then you may need to have a few different options in your gundog training toolbox. One of the most common issues that can occur is the lack of, or poor, delivery of retrieves and often it is quite simply down to the way in which the dog has been taught in the early stages of its training. Most well-bred gundogs will have a natural instinct to carry things around and the key is to get them to bring the items back to us, the handler, rather than run off and keep the 'treasure' for themselves. More often than not another contributing factor to a poor delivery is the handler's body language. It's not unusual for a novice handler to display behaviours of anxiety when their dog is coming back with a retrieve and dogs, being very perceptive to the handler's body language, may pick up on this and try and avoid coming directly back to the handler.

Whether you plan to run your gundog in scurries, working tests, field trials or work them in the shooting field as an all-round gundog you will want them to go out and smartly bring back their retrieves and deliver them

Right. A gundog that can deliver its retrieve 'to hand' swiftly and efficiently is a real benefit in the shooting field.

Above. Dogs are very perceptive to the handler's body language. Lifting your hands to waist height will encourage the dog to lift its head as it comes into you.

Right. Plenty of stroking around the dog's head will help to desensitise it which will help when the dog brings back a retrieve.

to hand. This is a fundamental part of a gundog's work. There is nothing more annoying and indeed frustrating than a dog that runs around you with a dummy or a bird in its mouth whilst you are trying desperately to get hold of it. It can also be quite embarrassing, especially if the dog is bringing back a pricked bird which needs dispatching as quickly as possible. It is also a question of efficiency as a dog that makes a swift and tidy delivery can then be set up and sent out for another retrieve. If you plan to shoot with your dog, whether at a peg, walked-up shooting or even in a hide, a good 'heads up' delivery means that you won't be swinging a (broken) gun around as you try and catch the dog to take a retrieve. Once a dog has got into the habit of messing around with its retrieve it will always be more problematic to cure, so it is better to take the correct steps early on to prevent this from happening in the first place. Elements of this training exercise can put a certain amount of pressure on the dog and so it is important that the dog is capable of dealing with this level of training.

There are a number of basics that need to be in place as you cannot expect to get a good delivery from your dog if it has not been trained to come and sit or stand in front of you, and this is the first piece of the jigsaw that needs to be put in place. As gundog trainers we can learn a lot from other 'dog discipline' trainers, especially the obedience handlers, and when training a gundog to come in nice and straight and lift its head up, some of their techniques can work really well.

Start by sitting the dog at a short distance from you and simply call him into you. Make sure you stand upright and don't lean towards the dog. The reason for keeping the distance short at this stage is so the dog doesn't have the opportunity to get up any speed and try to get past you. As the dog comes into you, keep your hands in front of you at waist height and just as the dog reaches you give the 'sit' command and slowly lift up your hands and this will cause the dog to bring his head up. Once the dog is sitting in front of you calmly stroke his head and chest. This has two purposes. The first is to encourage the dog to lift his head and the second is that it desensitises the dog to having your hands near its head, preventing the dog becoming 'hand-shy' which can cause the dog to move his head from side to side as you try and take a retrieve. Once you have your dog coming into you nice and straight, and he is quite used to sitting in front of you, the next stage is to introduce a retrieve.

Once your dog has the basic idea of going out and bringing back a retrieve you can begin to gradually build up the dog's keenness and confidence by making the retrieves slightly more challenging. You can still use the retrieving lane but by now your dog should be really keen to come directly back to you so you can move to a more open area, even if it is your garden. The basis of a memory retrieve is that the dummy or ball is thrown out so the

When introducing memory retrieves you can restrain your dog by either looping a lead around its neck or by simply holding the dog's chest.

dog can see it (a seen retrieve) and then either by virtue of the length of time you delay sending the dog or by turning or moving the dog, it loses its mark and it then must remember where the retrieve landed.

One important thing to remember is to always make sure that your dog is facing the direction that you want it to run out. You will often see handlers leaning right over a dog to send it out for a retrieve. This may look stylish, but in truth it is not very practical. If you are carrying a gun or have a game carrier full of pheasants hanging over your shoulder, you won't be able to strike that kind of pose without getting your barrels full of mud or smacking your dog around the head with a load of birds. Dogs have a wider field of vision than humans so they can easily see your hand giving a direction when you are standing up. Remember, we are aiming to train a dog for practical use in the shooting field and it is unlikely you will want to line your dog up for a 500-metre blind retrieve where pointing it in a very specific direction may be necessary.

Each time you begin an exercise it is worth thinking about any issues that may occur and when introducing a delayed memory retrieve to a dog there are a few things to watch out for. How they are dealt with will very much depend on the personality of your dog. First of all, up until this point you have been allowing the dog to run out quite quickly to pick up a retrieve and now you will be making it wait, which can be frustrating and confusing for the dog. This can induce whingeing and whining, which need to be avoided at all costs. This is where you will have to be able to read your dog and adjust your training accordingly. Secondly, don't be tempted to make things too difficult by increasing the distance of the memory retrieve too quickly. These early exercises are all about building up the dog's confidence.

The most basic way of introducing a memory retrieve is to restrain the dog, either on a lead or by holding it – depending on your dog's keenness you could either put your hand across the dog's chest or hold it in one arm. Throw out a retrieve and hold the dog back. The aim is not to send the dog until it relaxes. You may have to gently stroke the dog to settle it. Once you feel it relax you can send it for the retrieve. It is easier if you don't use a lead, as the action of taking off the lead can excite the dog and you can end up having a bit of a battle with it. However, if you do need to use a lead it can be better to loop it loosely around the dog's neck rather than putting it on properly. You can then just simply drop one end when you send the dog. It should now be obvious that not only are you introducing memory retrieves you are also beginning the process of steadying the dog, which is another important aspect of a gundog's training. As you progress with this exercise you can gradually extend the time and the distance before sending the dog for the retrieve.

There are another couple of techniques which can not only help to develop the memory retrieves but can also help to increase the keenness in the dog. Restrain the dog and throw out a retrieve, but this time just turn the dog away in the opposite direction and then turn back and send the dog. If you have one of the smaller breeds or are training a puppy you can pick up the dog when you turn around. The dog will momentarily lose its original mark on the retrieve so will have to remember where it saw it land. Once again you can gradually delay the time in turning back around before sending the dog.

Another way of introducing memory retrieves is to sit the dog up and if it is not steady yet, restrain it (either on the lead or by holding it) and throw out a dummy, turn the dog and walk it away from the retrieve. If you haven't done much lead work you can carry a smaller dog or puppy. Initially don't go too far, turn the dog and to begin with send it fairly quickly. As you progress you can turn the dog but delay the time before you send it, and you can increase the distance.

When developing the memory retrieve use a marked-out area and extend the time that you send the dog for each retrieve.

If you have a dog that has been trained with basic memory retrieve exercises, there are plenty more challenging tasks that can be used to either further the dog's training or to sharpen up existing skills and they are all applicable in a practical sense in the shooting field. When picking up with your dog it may well be in a situation where it must sit quietly for long periods of time and during a drive it will have to mark and remember where birds have landed and we can train for these situations, albeit artificially.

It is better if you can either mark out an area (plastic fence posts are ideal) or use a corner of a field. Ideally you want an area of rough cover, so the dog has to work for the retrieves rather than finding them by eye. Sit the dog up and throw into the area several small dummies or tennis balls: around six works quite well. The dog should be able to mark them all visually. Don't throw them too close together as you don't want to encourage the dog to swap retrieves. You then want to sit the dog next to you and wait.

One issue that can occur is that the handler will quite often unconsciously send the dog out at around the same time delay and the dog soon develops an internal clock and may get very twitchy or even run in when it gets to the time it has been used to being sent. If you can, set a timer on your mobile phone or just make a mental note of the time and make sure you

Do not always send your dog from your side especially if you are training one of the spaniel breeds.

Using the twelve and six o'clock positions is a good way of teaching your dog to trust you and to only retrieve what you want it to retrieve.

vary the time delay before sending the dog. After each retrieve, you will need to move your position. This not only makes the retrieve more challenging for the dog, but it also keeps them guessing and not pre-empting your next move. This also teaches them the vital lesson of switching off after each element of the exercise.

A variation on the above exercise is to use the corner of a field, throw in several retrieves whilst keeping the dog steady. You want to divide the area into a quadrant (like a piece of cake). Your first position to send the dog is from either the far left or right and then each time you move around in a semi-circle. This not only develops the dog's memory, but it also gives the dog experience in being sent at different angles and varying wind directions. The dog will now start to learn how to work with the wind. By using the corner of a field, you are restricting the dog to a specific area and by virtue of setting out a number of retrieves you will be building up the dog's confidence. Obviously once the dog has picked up most of the retrieves the remaining few get harder to find. If the dog struggles and begins to lose confidence call it back and throw a seen retrieve into the area and send the dog. You should find that once it has made a positive find it will have a bit more confidence to go back out again. You want the dog to learn and develop the mindset that if you have sent it out for a retrieve with your 'fetch' or 'out' command it should stick at the task until either it finds the dummy or you call it back. Remember: 'success will develop confidence'.

Just one point to note, most of the retrieving breeds will nearly always be sent out for a retrieve from the handler's side. However, a spaniel's job is to hunt and flush game away from the handler and will more often than not be sent from a short distance away from the handler. So when practising this exercise do not always send the dog from your side – occasionally move off to one side and send the dog. By doing this you are also beginning to introduce the early informal stages of left and right directional work.

Another memory retrieve exercise is based on using the twelve and six o'clock positions. It will help if you have a focal point around which you can throw your dummies: a tree or a plastic fence post will work. Stand in the middle of the 'clock' face and throw out a retrieve to the twelve and six o'clock positions. When throwing them out vary the distance you throw the retrieves as this will further test the dog. Take your time – these exercises are all about teaching the dog to mark and remember multiple retrieves; when you are ready send the dog but be prepared in case it tries to run past you on the way back to get to the opposite dummy. Mix and match which way you send your dog, don't fall into a pattern of sending it for opposite ends alternatively, keep your dog guessing and you will keep its focus.

At this point you may be thinking, 'Why is teaching this kind of retrieve important?' Well, from a practical point of view imagine this scenario. You shoot a bird out in front, and it falls dead, and your dog has a solid mark on the retrieve. Just as you go to send the dog another bird gets up and you shoot that one behind you, but it is pricked and runs. Through these training exercises you know you can deal with this situation. Your dog has been taught to trust you and so you can send him in the direction you want, not the direction the dog wants to go. By now you will have also gathered that as well as training the skill of memory retrieves you are also teaching it to make multiple retrieves, and this is important. All too often a novice trainer will only concentrate on sending the dog for single retrieves and this becomes the default for the dog. You will now have invertedly conditioned the dog to make one retrieve and think that is the end of the exercise and it doesn't believe you that there is another retrieve to make. Don't fall into that trap.

There will be occasions in the shooting field when you will have to send your dog for a retrieve that it hasn't seen. That could be because another Gun asks you to find a bird that they have shot or your dog has flushed a bird from within some deep cover and didn't have the chance to see it fall. This is known as a blind retrieve. By the time you get to this stage in your dog's retrieving training it should have complete and utter trust that when you use your command, and send the dog out, there is something for it to find. Now, obviously in the real world the dog may not always find the retrieve but in the early stages of training you must build up that trust and confidence by the dog consistently being successful, initially as a straightforward seen and

Teaching your gundog to run a straight line regardless of breed will really pay dividends in the shooting field.

then, as the dog's confidence grows, delayed memory retrieves. Bit by bit you are building the foundations of the dog's training and now is the time to move on to blind retrieves. Without wishing to sound like a stuck record, before you move on to these exercises your dog must have full confidence in your retrieving command. If you move on too quickly you are setting up your dog to fail and you need to avoid that at all costs. The chances are you will get frustrated when your dog struggles to complete the exercise and that will just feed back down to the dog and before you know it things are spiralling out of control.

Teaching a dog blind retrieves is basically fairly straightforward as it is all about confidence. Once again pick a corner of a field or some reference point such as a tree or plastic fence post. Over a period of a few training sessions give the dog some straightforward seen retrieves – obviously vary the angle and the distance you send the dog. Once the dog is confidently making these straightforward retrieves, leave it in your vehicle or keep it out of sight and place a retrieve in the same area you have been previously working in, collect the dog and get it set up in the way you have been doing during the previous training sessions and send it. You should find the dog will go straight to the area and make the retrieve. Practise this over a few sessions and not only vary the distance you send the dog but also the length of time before you get the dog out of your vehicle. If possible, you could even leave a retrieve out overnight.

Going back to the twelve and six o'clock memory exercise, this can also be used to build on blind retrieves. Set up a blind retrieve at one end of the clock face and then get the dog. Throw out a seen to the opposite point and then turn the dog away and send it for the previously set up blind retrieve. If your preceding lessons have been fully trained and understood the dog should trust you and go out for the blind. Initially, keep the distance to the blind fairly short so the dog has a good chance of finding the dummy. If the dog struggles just walk it a bit closer and set it up again. If you get success turn it back towards the seen, that has now in fact become a memory retrieve, and send the dog. As you progress with this exercise you can again increase the distance between the two retrieves but make sure you do this

Using a blue or high-contrast 'target' dummy will help to give your gundog confidence when teaching it to run a straight line.

When lining up your dog do not look at the target dummy. Watch the dog and as soon as it locks on send it with your retrieving command.

gradually. You don't want to increase the difficulty too quickly and cause the dog to fail. As the dog's confidence increases you can, of course, put out more than one blind retrieve and throw out more than one seen retrieve as a distraction: remember, constantly mix it up. Swap and change what you set up and how you send your dog – don't always send your dog from your side, especially if it is a spaniel.

If you ever get the chance to watch some of the top retriever handlers and their dogs when competing in a field trial you may well be in awe of the way the dogs are sent out for a long retrieve. The dog runs a straight line until such times that they either find the retrieve or are stopped and redirected. In practical terms it is unlikely that the vast majority of people that work their gundogs on shoots will ever need to send their dog in a 500-metre straight line. However, if you train your dog to run out even 100 metres in a straight line that will not only be really beneficial but more efficient. A common issue seen with many gundogs is when they are sent out for a retrieve, especially a blind retrieve, they run out about 20 to 25 metres and start hunting for the dummy. You can bet your bottom dollar that is the average distance the handler can throw a dummy and the dog has become conditioned to always finding its retrieve at that distance. This is why it is so important to vary the length of your retrieving exercises.

The best kind of training exercises are the ones that involve a number of different components and with this particular exercise you can practise walking to heel, sit (with whistle), steadiness, memory retrieves, picking multiple retrieves and learning to run a straight line. You will also be tapping into a bit of science in that you will be using the dog's visual ability. As previously mentioned our dogs see the world in a different way to humans and as trainers, we can use how they see both colour and contrast to initially teach them to run in a straight line. A few years ago, a new design of gundog training dummy was introduced. Called a 'target' dummy, it came in three colours: green, blue, and red, and all of them had a white band around the middle to create contrast (dark colour with a white band). There are now many variations of this original design, but all basically do the same thing.

**Swap and change what you set up and how you send your dog ...**

For this exercise you need a flat area and if you can find a track, so much the better. Initially just using one dummy, either walk the dog at heel with you or sit the dog and walk out about 20 metres and stand the dummy on its end. Depending on the kind of dummy you are using, if you struggle to get the dummy to stand up just stamp your heel into the ground to make a small dent and that will help. Set the dog up and do not look at the dummy. You must watch the dog, and you can use your hand to help guide him. At this point it must be said that in all likelihood you will have seen handlers bending low over their dogs when sending them out for retrieves, but as mentioned earlier this is not a practical stance to take when in the shooting field.

Above. If your gundog keeps looking up at you when setting it up, taking a few steps forward can encourage the dog to look forward towards the dummy.

Right. Gradually increase the number of dummies in the line and correspondingly increase the distance the dog has to run out.

What you are looking for is the point when you see the dog 'lock on' to the dummy. Timing is important and at that very moment you should send it with your retrieving command.

The next step is to use two dummies. Make sure they are not set up too close to each other as you do not want to encourage the dog to run from the first on to the second one. Set the first one up at 20 metres and the second at around 30 metres. It can be useful to use a blue and white dummy as your second one as this will be more visible to the dog and help to give it confidence, especially as you are increasing the distance. Set the dog up and again watch for the 'lock on' and send the dog. The trigger point to watch for is when the dog picks the first dummy. You need to be ready with your recall command or whistle: timing is important. Get the dog back and get it settled and line it up again. If you find the dog keeps looking at you try taking a step or two forward and this can help to get the dog to look forward. Watch for the 'lock on' again and send the dog. You should find that the dog catches on quite quickly that as soon as it looks forward you will send it. Keep the exercise at just two dummies for a few sessions and then it is time to not only increase the distance but also the number of retrieves that you set up. There is no limit to the number of retrieves that you can set up, but realistically you will need around five or six to get a distance of about 100 metres or so. Once the dog is confidently going out in a straight line and retrieving all the dummies you can try laying down the last one so the dog can't see it so easily.

Obviously, you and your gundog won't necessarily be working along

The swapping of retrieves is a highly undesirable trait in a gundog and is something that you should train to avoid happening.

Gradually bring in the two outside dummies and introduce a third to create a triangle. Your gundog should only pick one at a time.

a track or on flat grass when out in the shooting field, so at some point you will need to set up the exercise where the dog must run a line in rough cover or even through woodland. Before you progress to this your gundog must understand the principle of being sent out in a straight line, so don't be too keen and rush to the next stage. The way you set up the exercise is the same as before although it may be beneficial to use some kind of marker as to where the dummies have been set out. Plastic electric fence posts are ideal for this purpose. Remember each time you begin a new exercise go back to the beginning, so in this case you start off with one retrieve and build it up again. If at any time your dog decides it would rather go off hunting or runs offline, get it back and line it up and send it again. Don't let it get away with going off-piste. Also don't get involved in trying to handle the dog out to the retrieve. The exercise is running a straight line – it is not a handling exercise.

Begin by setting out the retrieves as straightforward memories by walking out with the dog and setting the dummies out by your markers. Start with one and then gradually build up to multiple retrieves. Once again when the dog has fully grasped the idea of running out in a straight line through cover you can then set up your blind retrieves. The more variation of ground cover you can train on the better. There is an old saying: 'Don't just train on the ground you have ... train on ground that you may have.' The more experience you can give your dog during its training the better it will be prepared for entering the shooting field.

Before beginning this exercise, you should ensure your dog's basic obedience is solid, especially as this is one of the more complex training exercises. Make sure your dog has a keen retrieving instinct, a good recall and understands the command 'leave it'. If any of these are not fully understood by the dog, then do not attempt to train these particular exercises as the potential is for the dog to get very confused and it may even refuse to retrieve. It is important to stay calm and make your commands clear and precise.

You will need two high-contrast dummies, so they are really visible to the dog. Sit the dog and set the two dummies at approximately ninety degrees to the left and right; do not set the dummies up too close to each other. Line up your dog and send it for one of the retrieves. As soon as the dog has the dummy in its mouth immediately recall it as you do not want it to run over the other dummy. Timing is key. Take the retrieve and put it back in place and then send the dog for the opposite one. The next stage is to gradually move the dummies closer together. Obviously as you reduce the distance there is a greater chance of the dog running over to the other retrieve. If this does happen get the dog back, preferably without the dummy and set the task up again. It is vital you get your timing perfect. As soon as the first dummy is picked give the dog lots of encouragement to get it back to you as quickly as possible.

Once your dog is consistently picking the angled dummies you can increase the difficulty and temptation. Set up three dummies in a triangle with the middle one nearest to you and the dog. By now your dog should have the idea that it should only pick the one dummy at a time, but do not be complacent. Get on the recall as soon as the dummy is in the dog's mouth.

The final stage in this exercise is to reverse the triangle and put the middle dummy farthest away from your sending point. This will mean the dog has to go through the two outer dummies and pick the middle one first. You will, of course, mix this up and change which dummy you want the dog to pick but initially concentrate on the middle one. When you are confident the lesson has been learnt you can try the same exercise using cold game but remember to set up the task from step one, treat it as a new lesson.

# 5. Heelwork

By constantly changing your direction when training heelwork and using a non-distracting training location you will find that the dog will have to concentrate on you as the handler.

Getting a gundog of any breed to walk on and off the lead at heel can be one of the biggest challenges you will face as a trainer, yet it is one of the fundamental requirements of a gundog's basic training. No matter what aspect of the shooting field you eventually want your gundog to be involved in it should walk next to you under control, on and off the lead, without either pulling on the lead or wandering off doing its own thing. It is normally accepted that the retrieving breeds should be well disciplined in the requirement of walking to heel, but even if you have a spaniel that you plan to work in the beating line it can be a real bonus and even a necessity to be able to call your dog into your side when working through cover crops such as maize, or when you reach a flushing point and you need to keep your dog under close control. You have only got to look at the numerous leads, harnesses and other 'quick fixes' that have been designed to make it more bearable for the owner to deal with a dog that is pulling when on a lead. It is a massive market and yet some time spent doing the basics can get most dogs walking properly on the lead.

There is a train of thought that putting a gundog on a lead too early can reduce some of its drive, particularly where spaniels are concerned, but the simple truth is that for the majority of owners getting their dog used to walking on a lead is an absolute necessity. Not everyone has the luxury of being able to put their dog in a vehicle, take it up to a wide-open space and let it out. Most people will have to walk the dog on a lead from an early age. However, teaching a dog to walk properly at heel doesn't have to start right from the first time they are able to go out. They need to be mature both physically and mentally to be able to deal with the restrictions that heelwork puts on a dog. As already mentioned, it is an important aspect of a gundog's training and apart from not having your arm pulled from its socket every time you go out, there are practical reasons as well. If you have one of the retrieving breeds and plan to use it as a peg dog, you will want it to walk nicely as you walk out to your peg. You will have your gun, cartridge bag and maybe even a stick and if you are also trying to hold on to a dog that is pulling you across the field it really can be quite challenging. If you are working a dog in the beating line, there will be plenty of times when you will need it to walk at heel next to you especially when putting a lead on is impractical such as being at the flushing point in thick cover or beating through maize.

...for the majority of owners getting their dog used to walking on a lead is an absolute necessity.

Heelwork training can be boring for both the handler and the dog, and it is something that you must be consistent with. Do not let your dog out of the car and let them pull all the way out to the training field and then proceed to do a session on heelwork and then let them pull all the way back. If you have to walk to your training area, make sure the dog knows what it

There is a right and a wrong way to put on a slip lead. The correct way is with the weighted part hanging down from the loop.

This is the wrong way to use a slip lead: the weighted part is above the loop.

has to do from the outset. Keep heelwork sessions short as they can be quite intense for the dog but try and train this every time you go out. It is easy to incorporate heelwork into many other aspects of the dog's training exercises. It can be really beneficial to do your heelwork in a car park or on some kind of tarmac: this will help to stop the dog trying to get its nose down and there will be fewer distractions.

With regard to the actual lead, generally gundogs do not wear collars when working so most handlers will use a standard slip lead. One of the most common mistakes is that handlers put the lead on the wrong way around. Putting the lead on incorrectly does have a detrimental effect on how the lead works. Quite simply the weighted part of the lead should be below the eye or loop as this allows the lead to slacken off when the lead is relaxed. The wrong way is to have the weighted part of the lead above the eye or slip. This way when the lead is tightened, the lead around the dog's neck will not slacken back off and it can lead to choking. Practise putting the lead on and taking it off your dog the right way, so it becomes second nature to you.

One of the most effective ways of getting your dog to understand heelwork is to work in lots of tight circles or figures of eight. Doing this means the dog has to concentrate on what is going on and be more attentive to your body language. If you just walk in straight lines, the dog can quickly switch off the task and on to more interesting things such as sniffing the ground. The other advantage of this method is that you are leading the dog sideways which helps to prevent it pulling forward as it is slightly off balance.

Another technique that you can use to keep the dog's concentration is to occasionally stop and take a few steps back. Basically like a lot of aspects of a gundog's training keep them guessing as to what you are going to do next: that way they can never second-guess you. Make sure you do change directions: practise both clockwise and anticlockwise.

A common question is where the dog's body position should be when walking at heel. Ideally you want to have their front feet in around about the same place as yours with their head just slightly forward of your leg. This will give you a good reference point, but it also allows the dog to have good forward vision which if you have a retrieving breed will pay dividends if you plan to do any walked-up shooting in the future. Quite often when you start out doing heelwork your dog may want to pull away from you and this can not only be annoying it can be the beginning of a bad habit forming. If this is the case, try and find a fence line or another barrier that you can walk the dog next to. This will help to prevent it wandering off to one side. Once the dog has got the idea and a good position is ingrained you can then move out onto more open ground.

Once you have your dog correctly walking to heel on the lead it is time to begin the transition to free-heelwork. Rather than dropping the lead on the floor which can get caught up in the dog's legs, you can either wrap the slip lead around the dog's neck or use a short slip lead with a knot in so you can hold it and when ready simply let go. The dog basically thinks it

Ideally the dog should be positioned with their feet in line with the handler's feet.

is still on the lead and attached to the handler: should the dog pull forward it is easy to get hold of and correct the dog. The final stage is, of course, to take the dog off the lead completely, but always maintain a series of ongoing heelwork exercises as previously described until you are confident the dog understands where it needs to be.

If the dog pulls off to one side when teaching heelwork it can be beneficial to find a fence line or another barrier to walk the dog alongside.

The use of a short lead known as a 'heeling lead' can be a good intermediate step from proper lead work to free-heelwork.

# 6. Marking

If you are hoping to train your gundog to be proficient in all aspects of the shooting field, it will need to have the ability to mark shot game. It is a skill that all gundogs need to develop and, if you are lucky, some dogs seem to have the uncanny and natural ability to know where a retrieve has landed but others will need to be trained. If you plan to shoot over your dog or go picking up with it, 'marking' becomes a vital skill. To be able to give the command 'mark' and for the dog to know and understand that it needs to look forward for a potential retrieve will help to ensure that you get an efficient and quick retrieve which is especially important if you need to pick a running bird. When a dog is hunting and pushes a rabbit out of some rushes, it often won't see it run and therefore can't get a visual mark on any potential retrieve. Now when it is sent it will often get its nose down and follow the scent trail. On the other hand, when hunting feathered game, the bird will flush and fly and unless the bird is pricked and runs on the ground, there will be no scent line directly to the retrieve. This means that unless the dog has been trained and has learnt to watch (mark) the bird away, the retrieve will be much more challenging.

There are lots of reasons why you should teach your gundog to mark, but the main one is it enables you to get the dog quickly out to a retrieve. If you do plan to enter any working tests or indeed trials this is an essential skill and can make the difference between winning and losing. Even if you have no desire to enter any competitions and just want to work your dog in the shooting field, especially when picking up, a dog that can mark fallen game and remember where it fell will be far more efficient in sweeping up at the end of a drive. If you plan to shoot over your dog on a rough or walked-up day, then the ability of a dog to watch a flushed pheasant or a bolted rabbit away will enable you to send it for any possible retrieve and it will go straight to the point of fall without running all over the place and spoiling other ground that may be holding game. The bottom line is that you should try and ensure that any game, especially injured game, is retrieved quickly and dispatched humanely. One thing to bear in mind is that the dog's eye level is significantly lower than the handler's and quite often a young inexperienced dog will 'mark short' and run out to a retrieve but begin to hunt for it before it has reached the fall area. This can be overcome by training, but it is something to be aware of and if need be to make allowances for by moving forward with the dog until it has gained experience and is able to judge distances more consistently.

> **... a dog that can mark fallen game and remember where it fell will be far more efficient in sweeping up at the end of a drive.**

Marking the fall of a retrieve is something that can be developed from an early age. Even when you are throwing out retrieves for a young pup they are learning to watch where the ball lands. Some dogs will do this quite naturally and you will develop this further as the dog goes through

Remember your gundog's eye level is a lot lower than yours so bear this in mind when setting up marking exercises.

its training, others may need guidance and encouragement. Now you have an understanding of how a dog uses its eyes, you can once again use this knowledge to your advantage when teaching your dog marking exercises. Another factor to be considered is how acute a dog's hearing is and how that can also be developed when training a dog to mark. Ultimately, you need your gundog to use its senses: sight, scent, and hearing all play a part when a dog is marking a retrieve. Imagine you are picking up in a wood and birds are being shot and falling through the trees. Quite often the dog will not be able to see the bird but will hear the fall. You can help to develop this skill by training for such eventualities.

There is a distinct advantage in having a dog that can watch a bird as it is shot and lands. It will make the retrieve more efficient and helps to ensure that any injured game is quickly returned to the handler so it can be humanely dispatched. In the early stages of teaching a dog to mark, the colour choice of dummy can really help the dog to see the retrieve more clearly. Just to recap, dogs see colour in a totally different way to humans and in the early stages of training either a blue or purple dummy will really stand out to a dog whereas a green or orange dummy can be more difficult for the dog to see. A high-contrast coloured dummy, such as black and white or blue and white will really stand out and can help to quickly build a young dog's confidence. Dummies with 'tails' or 'wings' on them are also very visible to a dog as the additions give some further movement and noise to the retrieve as it is thrown.

Not everyone has the luxury of being able to train with someone else or even have someone to throw dummies for them and this can create a few problems. However, with a few simple techniques these issues can be overcome. One problem that you may come across when training a dog to mark and you train on your own is that the dog will watch the dummy being thrown out but will then turn and look back at the handler, losing the mark on the retrieve. Good eye contact is a very desirable trait in a gundog but in this case, it is better that the dog keeps watching where the dummy has landed until it is sent.

The easiest way to overcome this is to sit the dog up and take a few steps forward in front of the dog and throw out the dummy. The dog will be naturally looking at you, the handler, and as a result its eyeline will already be forward in the direction of the retrieve. At this stage you can also introduce the command 'mark'. To start with, send the dog from where you have thrown the dummy. There are two reasons for doing this. The first is it encourages the dog to take a straight line to the retrieve without looking at you, the handler. The second reason is that if you have one of the spaniel breeds and you plan to shoot over it, quite often you will have to send the dog when it is hunting and flushing away from you and not right by your side, so you are in fact getting the dog used to that situation. An important aspect of this exercise is that you must not send the dog until he is looking out towards the dummy. If you get your timing right the dog soon learns that as soon as he looks out, he will get sent. Timing really is the key. If you have a dog that constantly looks at you, another method that can be employed is to throw the dummy into an open bush or against the trunk of a tree and quite often the noise will make the dog look around and again timing is critical. Send the dog as soon as he looks around towards the noise.

If you are fortunate enough to have someone that can come out and help you train you will still need to have a bit of planning in place. As has already been mentioned dogs see particular colours better than others and they are also very good at seeing contrast. If you are going to use a dummy thrower, think about the background before setting up the exercise. If you have a lot of trees or bushes behind the thrower the dog may not be able to see the dummy very well. Initially try and use a clear skyline and get your dummy thrower to launch the dummy high in the air so it stands out clearly against the sky. Obviously, you don't want to be using a very light-coloured dummy for the retrieve, a dark or two-tone one will stand out far better. Remember at this stage it is all about helping the dog to gain in confidence. We want it to succeed as often as possible. You must still use the command 'mark' as the dummy is thrown, and you will find that the movement from the thrower is quite often enough to draw the dog's eyeline. Initially, send the

**Ultimately, you need your gundog to use its senses: sight, scent, and hearing …**

Below right. With a young gundog it is better to ensure that they have a clear and highly visible view of any retrieve that is thrown. A high-contrast dummy with a clear skyline is ideal.

Below. A retrieve that is thrown against the backdrop of a tree line will be far more challenging for a dog to mark.

dog quite quickly as this helps the success rate of the dog getting straight to the fall. As the dog gains in experience you can then move to heavier cover and woodland, but remember each time you introduce a new scenario to the dog make the first few exercises straightforward and then gradually make the exercise more challenging.

Most marking by the dog will be done visually, but imagine a situation where your dog is working in dense cover such as bramble or laid bracken, it flushes a bird and it gets shot, the dog is unsighted due to the cover so what do you do? When working, a gundog will make use of three of its senses: smell, sight, sound and in this scenario, it is the last one that you want the dog to use. If you have trained your dog to mark the fall of a retrieve by

sound this puts you at a distinct advantage – you can send your dog from the point of the flush, and the dog should head straight for the area it heard the noise and then its nose will take over. The following exercises need to be practised so that the dog not only grows in confidence but by using different locations it will also gain experience in dealing with different scenarios.

As with all your training you want the dog to succeed in the task, so you will gradually build up the complexity of the exercise. Find an area of rough grass so the dummy will not be easily seen, use a heavy dummy so when it lands it does make a bit of a thump. Sit the dog next to you and put your hands over the dog's eyes. If you struggle to do this ask someone else to throw out the dummy. In the first instance do not throw the retrieve too far, and throw it out directly in front. As soon as the dummy lands send the dog, repeat this a few times and then try throwing the dummy off to one side. You may find the dog goes back to the initial spot and if it does call the dog back and try again until it realises that the noise will correspond to a retrieve.

Once your dog is confident in finding retrieves in rough grass you can move on to a different location and scenario. Find a suitable tree, preferably one with a large trunk and some rough cover around the base, and once

Teaching a gundog to mark by sound will give it a distinct advantage when out in the shooting field.

again sit the dog next to you and cover its eyes. The aim is to hit the trunk of the tree with the dummy and, if your aim is not great, get someone else to do it for you. The chances are the dummy will hit the trunk and fall straight down in the cover. This in fact is quite a difficult retrieve as any wind (scent) will be swirling around the base of the trunk. The noise should draw the dog to the tree and then it will have to work it out by using its nose. As the dog grows in confidence change the angle and distance of the retrieve.

In a real-life situation, the chances are that your dog will be marking by sound when working in cover and the retrieve will have also fallen into cover, so at some point we must train for this scenario. A loose stick pile is ideal to begin with, which will mean that the dummy can fall to the ground easily. Obviously the noise will be different from the rough grass and the tree trunk, so you are teaching the dog to associate retrieve with different noises. Simply repeat the exercise as you have done previously and do change angles and distance so any scent is blown in different directions.

A slight variation on this exercise is to throw a dummy into a stick pile but aim to get it hung up off the ground – it would not be unusual for a bird to get caught up like this. Initially, the dog will hunt the ground trying to locate the retrieve, and quite often they will be right underneath it. Give plenty of encouragement and eventually he will lift his head and find the dummy. It will be a good lesson learnt. Every now and again repeat this exercise in different locations and rest assured it will pay dividends at some point during a shoot day.

Train for any situation. It isn't unusual for a retrieve to get caught up off the ground and you can replicate this in your training programme.

# 7. Hunting

When hunting, a gundog should work within the effective range of a shotgun.

Hunting is a core skill that you and your gundog will have to master. As a trainer you may have done some research on this subject and, no doubt, you will have discovered that there are numerous views on how and when to teach your dog to hunt.

At this point it is important to clarify a few things. Trainers that are planning to compete in field trials with their dogs will encourage their young dogs to hunt from a very early age as they want to develop drive and pace in the dog. Basically, they are looking for the equivalent of a Ferrari and they will put in the control at a later stage, whereas a less skilled trainer may need to have a higher degree of control over the dog before unlocking the hunting mode. You may have also come across the phrase 'free-hunting'. This is where the dog is basically allowed the freedom to hunt on its own accord and, as a consequence, it quickly learns to hunt for itself and not in partnership with the handler. If allowed to develop this can be really challenging to rectify. Imagine the scenario where you take your dog out for a walk, you let it off the lead and it runs off up the field hunting along a hedge, it flushes a bird and gives chase. The dog has self-rewarded itself. This is then repeated over the next few walks and now the dog has no interest in you: it has learnt that all the fun is 100 metres along the hedge, and this quickly becomes its default behaviour. Basically you have now lost all control over your gundog.

What ground you have available to train on may dictate how you go about teaching and developing your gundog's hunting skills. Not everyone has access to rough cover or 'scenty' ground, but if you are dedicated to training your gundog at some point you will need to find some suitable ground. It doesn't have to be a 100-acre field: an unkept corner of the local park or a public wood can both work. You may just have to be a bit more imaginative in setting up your training exercises. In fact too much scent can be detrimental in the early stages, and you certainly need to keep away from areas where you may come across any pheasants or ground game. If you do feel that you need a bit of scent on the ground to get your dog hunting a bit better, then get some cold game or look out for a roadkill rabbit or pheasant and rub that over the area you want to hunt your dog. You could even buy some game scent from your gundog kit supplier and put that on a dummy and then rub that over the cover. Don't make excuses for your lack of facilities – you just have to be inventive and sometimes think outside the box.

**... too much scent can be detrimental in the early stages.**

A spaniel's hunting pattern is something that is quite often discussed amongst gundog trainers and although there are various interpretations regarding hunting patterns the one common factor is that the dog must hunt efficiently. Now, whether that is in what has become commonly known as a

Throwing a handful of grass to the opposite side will draw the dog's eyeline away from the fur ball being picked up by the handler.

windscreen wiper pattern or a more open quartering pattern, the dog needs to hunt within the killing range of a shotgun and that is around 30 to 40 metres. The dog therefore needs to be hunting no further than around 25 metres either side of the handler. The principle is that by the time you have mounted your gun to any game that is flushed, the target will still be within range to be shot. However, if the dog is hunting further away the quarry will be quickly out of range. The dog should hunt in an effective manner covering both sides of the handler: this is known as quartering. When working your dog in the beating line, birds will naturally run on in front and the dog will inevitably pull on the foot scent. If it has been trained to work close you will be able to keep on top of it and keep it under control, but this is not so easy if the dog has learnt the habit of hunting way out in front of the handler.

In the early stages of training your dog to hunt you will be aiming to get him questing in an area right around your feet. This is a lot closer than it will eventually be hunting, but it will soon pull out once it gets a few live game flushes and some fresh scent under its nose. Ideally you will want to practise this exercise on an area of rough grass, and it works better if there is little or no scent about as you need to concentrate the dog's work in a relatively tight area. You will also need a fur or a tennis ball to not only create interest for the dog, but to add a little bit of scent on the ground which will help to get the dog interested. If possible, always try and work the dog into the wind as this will help to keep them close.

Some dogs are reluctant to hunt ground that has no scent to get them fired up and not everyone has access to 'scenty' ground so this technique can help overcome the problem. Sit the dog up – it needs to be steady for this to work – and show it a ball. You can either rub it in the grass or you can even kick it about. This has two functions, it not only excites the dog, but it will also leave little pockets of scent, which in turn will help to get the dog's nose on the ground and help to hold it in the area. If you have a helper, you can shield the dog's eyes and get them to pick up the ball. However, if you are on your own a clever little trick is to grab a handful of grass and throw it out to one side and at the same time pick up the ball with your other hand. The grass will draw the dog's eye away from your hand that is picking up the ball.

As soon as you have picked up the ball, click off your dog to start it hunting. It is important that at this stage you hold your ground: if the dog pulls forward take a few steps back and encourage the dog back towards you. The theory behind this exercise is that the dog believes the ball is still in the grass and therefore will get its nose down and really start hunting for it. The dog will naturally be hunting near you and is unlikely to pull out as the limited scent and the visual indication are all in the same area. The key element to

Once the dog is hunting drop the ball off to one side. Do not let the dog see you do this as it can encourage the dog to anticipate what is going to happen.

Pip the dog back and indicate the area where you dropped the retrieve with a low hand indication.

this exercise is when the dog isn't looking, drop the ball right in close to you and call or pip (with the whistle) the dog back towards you and indicate with a low hand signal. The dog will find the fur ball and then you can get it to make a nice delivery. Once the dog has learnt the game you can move to a new area and repeat the exercise. Gradually over a period of a few days the dog's hunting pattern will build up and it will realise that if it stays close to you it will find something good, namely the ball. Hunting at this stage of the dog's training is all about having fun, and the overall key to any technique you decide to use is that the dog always finds or gets its reward close to you, the handler. You want to develop the total belief that the dog thinks that you are the provider of all good things. The theory behind this is that you reduce the desire in the dog to disappear over the horizon to self-hunt and, even worse, get a flush and a chase and therefore self-reward. By now you should have realised that you need to have developed a strong retrieving instinct in your gundog to enable you to further develop the dog's hunting technique. If your dog isn't interested in a dummy or ball, you really will have your work cut out to get it to hunt with you.

Another hunting exercise that taps into the desire to find and retrieve a ball or dummy is to find an area of rough cover and whilst leaving the dog in your vehicle or out of sight, place out a number of balls or small dummies. It is best to hide them in the cover rather than leave them visible as this will encourage the dog to get its nose down. Remember you can use red balls or dummies to make it even more testing for the dog. You need to spread out the retrieves. Fetch the dog and set it up as in the previous exercise and click it off hunting. This time you are going to move forward slowly in a zigzag pattern. Each time the dog casts off to one side turn your body in the opposite direction and call or pip the dog. It should run across you and then you turn back again in the opposite direction. If the dog indicates with its body language that it is finding scent don't be too quick to call it off as it may have located one of the balls you have set out. If the dog does find a ball, take it and cast the dog off again. Gradually build this exercise up over a period of sessions on the same ground and you will be surprised how quickly the dog learns to work either side of you - basically you are playing a simple game of 'hide and seek'.

Your body language and movement will have a direct effect on the reaction of the dog. Eventually you will aim to reduce the amount of turn whistles and cut down the zigzag pattern just relying on the turn of your shoulders to bring the dog back across your body. You may also find that your dog gets overly excited when you use your hand to indicate the area to hunt. Some dogs may even jump and try to nip the hand. If this happens, simply put your hands in your pockets and exaggerate your shoulder movement as you cast off the dog. In most cases this will work and stop the dog from jumping up.

Once you have got your gundog hunting a nice pattern in open but rough cover, it is time to encourage it to hunt thicker cover such as stick piles and patches of brambles. This kind of cover is a haven for game birds and once a dog has had a few positive finds in a thick stick pile or a heavy patch of bramble it will be more than willing to get stuck in; but initially the dog may be less than keen. If you are not careful you can put a young inexperienced dog off wanting to explore thicker cover as a young dog can be 'overfaced' by the trainer due to trying or even forcing it to go into bramble or heavy

When hunting your dog move your shoulders and turn in the opposite direction the dog is casting. This will encourage it to turn and develop a 'pattern'.

stick piles. As with all aspects of gundog training, the foundations should be built upon gradually and if you try and push a dog too quickly or give it tasks that it is not mentally and physically ready to cope with you will create future problems. Dogs need to be stimulated and if they are repeatedly sent into cover without any reward, such as a flush or a retrieve, they can quickly learn that there is no point to thrashing around in a bramble bush for no reward and they can become very reluctant to enter any cover. Just a word of caution, any gundog no matter how well bred will not continually hunt any cover without some kind of reward.

You will need to find or make some loose stick piles – at this stage you don't want to make them too dense – then sit the dog up and throw a tennis ball or even better a fur-covered ball into the sticks. You want the dog to see you do this. Walk away from the cover and hunt the dog back up to the sticks and then encourage the dog to 'get in'. With any luck, it will get into the sticks and find the ball. At this stage, you are teaching the dog to associate the command 'get in' with him finding something positive. Don't forget dogs learn by repetition, so over a number of training sessions repeat this exercise, if possible in different stick piles.

Don't forget dogs learn by repetition ...

By the time you get to this stage your dog should have total belief in you and that 'get in' command and you can now start to introduce it to heavier cover, gradually building up to heavier stick piles, loose bramble and perhaps even gorse bushes. Still make sure your dog is finding something good in the cover: hard rubber balls or small heavy dummies are good to use as they penetrate the cover a bit deeper than a tennis ball. If you have taken things gradually and slowly built up the dog's confidence, it should at this point really have connected that any form of cover could hold something good, and as time goes on and the dog has more finds you will find that it will be more willing to hunt out these likely spots by itself.

One of the most challenging hunting tasks you can undertake with your gundog will be to hunt hedges or ditches. If done correctly it can be highly effective in producing game especially when shooting over a gundog. If done incorrectly however it can be a total nightmare for the handler, although the dog may well be thoroughly enjoying itself! In the first instance it is important to understand why a hedge line or a ditch can be so difficult to work properly and the problems that can be encountered when working them.

Hedges and ditches are used by both feathered and fur game as natural, safe highways. Pheasants in particular will travel along the bottom of a hedge and if given the option would rather run than fly, and herein lies the problem for the gundog handler. Put a dog into a hedge and the chances are, unless you have both trained it and understand how to work it, the dog will disappear at a fast rate of knots. The dog will be following the foot scent of any fleeing game and more often than not will only reappear a few hundred metres further down the hedge when a bird decides to flush. This is not only undesirable in terms of any game being well out of range of a shot, but also if you are beating it can potentially put the dog nearer any flushing point with little or no chance of you, as the handler, having any control over the dog.

It is best to avoid working any novice gundog in a hedge or ditch until the dog is coming towards the end of its formal training. You need to have trust in the dog, and it needs to have a good hunting pattern instilled along with a complete understanding of the turn whistle. It is very difficult to correct a dog if it does decide to do a runner when it is inside a hedge, but you must be insistent that when you pip it back it responds. Initially, try to find a hedge with a stock fence on one side. You obviously hunt the open side as this prevents the dog from getting out the backside and disappearing with no chance of you catching it. Also, when training try to always work into the wind or the downwind side of the hedge; this will help to hold the dog.

Once you have found a suitable hedge or ditch line you can set about training your gundog to hunt it efficiently and under control. One mistake novice handlers make is that they stand too close to the cover when working

When hunting a hedge or a ditch, position yourself away from the cover as this will give you a better angle to see the dog working.

the dog and this limits your forward view of where the dog is: it's all about angles. You need to position yourself so you can see the dog in the hedge or ditch at a distance of about 10 metres. Also if you are shooting over your dog by being slightly further out it will make any potential shot easier. When casting off your dog remember it needs to go in at right angles to your position and not take off along the outside.

The technique for working a hedge or ditch is known as 'stitching', and although it does introduce an element of hunting over the same area it is the most effective way of working. Follow the dog as it works along the hedge and after about 10 metres stop it and pull it back with a turn whistle. As it comes back to you feed it back into the hedge and then move on and repeat. Think of this as a sewing stitch or as a loop. This way you are always in touch with the dog and not allowing it to pull too far forward.

For obvious reasons don't train this exercise in a dense hedge line or a thick, overgrown ditch where you can't see the dog, as the chances are it will take full advantage and get away from you. As you get more confident, and the dog knows what is expected, you can then gradually move on to thicker cover. One thing to point out is that in early spring nettles can be a real nuisance and they can put off a young dog, so just check the ground before beginning your training session. Although you will be concentrating on hunting the hedge, remember to also cover any ground the opposite side. Obviously, if this were a ploughed field you wouldn't expect your dog to hunt that, but if the area is rough grass or cover crops make sure you explore that as well as there will be a good chance that a rabbit or pheasant may well be tucked up in the cover.

At some point in your gundog's training, you will need to introduce your dog to live game and to what is known as 'hot scent'. This is an exercise that really does need some careful thought and planning if you are to avoid creating a whole set of new problems. There are a number of ways that you can do this. If you have a friendly gamekeeper, you may be able to get permission to walk around the feed rides when the poults are out and about, or you may be able to find an area where rabbits sit out alongside a hedgerow. However, by far the best way to introduce your dog to the excitement of live game is to use a rabbit pen. For those who are not sure what a rabbit pen consists of, it is basically a large, fenced area with plenty of rough grass, brashings, or stick piles to give the rabbits plenty of cover. Although they are called rabbit pens you may find that they may also contain a few pheasants, partridges or even the odd chicken. The use of a pen has two functions. The first is to take your dog's steadiness to a higher level and the second is so that you can

Work the cover in small chunks, 'stop' pip the dog back to you and feed it back into the hedge or ditch thus creating a 'stitching' pattern.

begin to develop the dog's hunting on scent under strict control and in a confined area. The dog will also have the opportunity to start the process of connecting the live quarry with scent, which is a vital aspect of a young dog's development.

There is no doubt that the introduction to live game in a rabbit pen can be fraught with potential problems and you should always assess a dog's personality and level of training before introducing it to the pen. It must be emphasised that unless you are experienced it is strongly suggested that you book a few lessons in a rabbit pen with a professional trainer – that way you will get some good advice and hopefully prevent any problems. There are pens that you can hire by the hour, and this may be an option. A young dog that has shown in relatively sterile conditions (no scent) that it has plenty of drive and is what would be called 'hard going' will need a different approach to a dog that needs a bit of geeing up. A dog lacking in pace may need or even be encouraged to have a little chase of something it has flushed, and it is quite surprising how a dog changes and goes up a few gears once it has been stimulated in this way. On the other hand, a harder hunting dog may well need reining in a little bit and need tighter control. The following exercises are built up over several visits to the pen: don't hurry this process.

At some point you will have to introduce your gundog to the excitement of 'hot scent'. A feed ride, release pen or rabbit pen is the ideal location.

The freshly vacated 'seat' of a rabbit is guaranteed to get any gundog excited.

Initially, introduce the dog to the pen on a lead and walk it around until you can see a rabbit tucked up in a patch of rough grass. Ideally, you don't want to have too many stick piles in the pen in the early stages as you want the dog to see the flush to start developing the game/scent connection. Once you have found a rabbit and it flushes, immediately stop, and get the dog to sit using a combination of the whistle and if need be the verbal 'sit' command. Standing is not acceptable. Do not be concerned where the rabbit has gone: concentrate on the dog. You may well find that the first flush will not get much of a reaction but beware as this will change on subsequent finds. Give the command 'gone away' and walk in the opposite direction. This helps to instil into the dog that he should not take off after the rabbit when asked to 'move on' or 'hunt on'.

Try and find a few more rabbits and once you are satisfied that the dog is getting the idea you can then encourage it to get its nose down in the area that the rabbit has just left. This is known as a 'seat'. Quite often the dog will be more interested in pulling off in the direction the rabbit ran off, but by using a low hand indication and plenty of verbal encouragement you will hopefully find that they get the idea, and the change in a young dog when it gets the fresh scent of game is quite incredible. At this stage, the dog is still on a lead. After a few sessions where the dog has been on a short lead and under direct physical control you can tie two leads together or use a long line to allow the dog a bit more 'freedom' to hunt. The aim is to allow the dog to make a find and flush further away from the handler and to stop and sit to the whistle and flush. If the dog breaks and attempts to run in you will have to go back a few steps and use the short lead again. If you have success leave the dog sitting and think about what just happened. This is a really important aspect of this exercise: not only does it give the dog time to relax and calm down, it also gives the handler a chance to gather their thoughts.

When you are quite happy that the dog is getting the idea, remove the lead and let it free-hunt. However, before you allow the dog to do this, clear a corner of the pen of any rabbits as at this stage you only want the dog to be hunting fresh scent and learning to get its nose down. By using the corner of the pen, you are limiting the hunting area and as a result you will have a bit more control over the dog.

Once you are confident that your dog has made enough progress you can move on to hunting it in more open areas of the pen and hopefully get a flush or two. One piece of advice is to just watch out for rabbits sitting up against the pen wire as quite often when they flush, they will run in a straight line along the fence, and this is very tempting for any dog. If your dog does give chase you need to get out after it, catch it, bring it back to the point of the flush and give it a firm 'sit' command. If you have done your basic training right the dog will understand what that means.

Consistency is the most important thing. Hunt, flush, sit/stop should become the normal pattern of behaviour for your dog and if you gradually build up the dog's experience this will all fall into place. Rabbit pens are great training aids, but they can also be overused – dogs soon learn to hunt from stick pile to stick pile and lose any hunting pattern. They can also become sticky in their hunting especially if there is too much game in the pen. It is better that they learn to hunt to find their quarry rather than falling over it.

# 8. Introducing Whistle Commands

A young puppy will see you as the centre of its world ... until teenage hormones set in!

People quite often ask, 'When is the best time to start using a whistle?' Well in truth there isn't a right or wrong time, but if you do use the place board exercises to teach your gundog the basics then it is relatively straightforward to introduce both the 'sit' command and recall whistle without the dog even knowing it is being taught the exercise.

By far the most common whistle used in the gundog world is the Acme plastic whistle. These come in various pitches and although you can use any model for your dog, generally spaniel handlers use a 210½ and retriever handlers use a 211½. The 210½ is quieter and therefore is better for close-up dog work whereas the sound from a 211½ carries further and is more suitable for dogs that will be working at a distance. One piece of practical advice is to buy a couple of whistles and always keep a spare in your vehicle. You wouldn't be the first person to head off training and realise that you have left your whistle at home.

For some novice trainers using a whistle doesn't necessarily come naturally and may need a bit of practice. First of all, it is better if you hold the whistle with your teeth rather than between your lips. If you are new to this, you may also need to practise giving verbal commands whilst holding the whistle in your mouth. It's not easy but as your training progresses you will soon realise that this is a useful skill to have learnt. Get into the habit of 'whistle in ... lead off'. Your whistle, and the commands associated with it, will eventually become your brakes and your steering wheel and therefore you should be able to use it as soon as your dog's lead has been removed. A classic scenario is that you are waiting at the beginning of a drive on your very first shoot day, and you have your little dog sitting nicely on the lead next to you. The time comes to begin beating and you slip off the lead and cast the dog off. He immediately flushes a rabbit and begins to chase, and you need to stop him. However, you have forgotten the golden rule 'whistle in ... lead off' and you are now trying desperately to find your whistle that is tucked underneath various items of clothing. You will only do it once!

**... buy a couple of whistles and always keep a spare in your vehicle.**

Without any doubt one of the issues that causes novice trainers the most sleepless nights is training the sit/stop whistle. Get it right and you will have a high degree of control over even the hardest-going dog; get it wrong and the wheels can come off very quickly and it can not only be a huge embarrassment but may result in you being told never to return to a particular shoot. The stop whistle is the brake on your dog. When you use that single sharp blast, the dog needs to respond immediately. It needs to stop running or hunting and preferably spin round and look at the handler ready to respond to the next command. To some it can seem to be a complicated process but like so many aspects of gundog training if you lay down your foundations properly it will make the ongoing exercises so much easier.

Before covering the basic steps, it should be pointed out that the single blast on your whistle can be called the 'stop', the 'sit', or in certain circumstances the 'look at me' whistle. No matter what you call it they all mean the same thing and the dog must be taught to react quickly. A sharp stop whistle is a joy to watch, a sloppy one is like watching an oil tanker trying to slow down ... it takes forever. One common failing is that the dog either ignores or at the least is very sloppy on the stop whistle. Often this is because the handler has been using the command without any reward for the dog or any reaction from the handler. Consequently, the dog develops the attitude of 'What's the point of stopping? Nothing is going to happen' and basically they get bored. You need to develop a behaviour in the dog so when it hears the whistle, the dog will want to stop and look at the handler because something positive is going to happen.

During your gundog's shooting career, you will need to stop it in mid-action hundreds if not thousands of times. It needs to stop when flushing birds or ground game, it needs to stop when out on a retrieve and you have to redirect it; you may need to stop it from running in, you may just need to stop it from heading towards a potentially dangerous situation. The stop whistle is the ultimate command, and it is the single most important thing you can teach your gundog from a relatively early age. Alongside the audible command you will also be introducing a physical indication with your hand to help reinforce the instruction. This is especially important when working your dog at a distance. As with all hand signals you must make sure they are clear and there is separation between your arm and hand and your face and body. When initially teaching the sit whistle also position your arm high above your head and slightly off to one side with your palm facing outwards. This helps to give a clear signal even at a distance.

Dogs learn by repetition and association, basically by doing an exercise over and over that then becomes a behaviour. So, if we take this logic in terms of introducing the sit whistle, you have already taught and conditioned the dog to come and sit on a place board in front of you, which has now become an ingrained habit and you should be at the point where the dog is doing this without even receiving a verbal command. Now all you have to do is introduce a single pip on the whistle as the dog comes and sits on the board. The dog will quickly associate the pip of the whistle with the action of sitting, which it always does when it gets on the place board. This is a far kinder and more effective way of introducing a sit whistle than the old-school way of having the dog on a lead and giving it a tug every time the whistle is blown.

If you haven't used a place board for your training, there are other ways of introducing the sit whistle. One of the first things people teach their

Left. Always make sure your hand signals are clear and precise as you will eventually be directing your gundog at a distance.

Right. There needs to be plenty of separation between your hand/arm and your body.

pup is to sit at feed time. Simply lift the bowl slowly above the pup's head and they will sit on the floor. Now you can initially introduce the verbal 'sit' command but once the pup has connected that with the act of sitting you simply follow it with a single short pip on the whistle. Gradually the pup connects the noise with the required behaviour which is to sit.

The traditional way of introducing the stop whistle is to have the dog on a lead and walking next to you. Every time you stop, give a verbal 'sit' command once the dog understands this you then introduce the single pip of the whistle. You must make sure the dog sits straight away. This method certainly works especially if you haven't had the chance to condition the dog from the puppy stage. Remember to give the dog plenty of praise when it gets it right and as you progress try changing your pace with the dog at heel and this can help to keep the dog's focus and concentration. You must not let the dog get away with ignoring the command; you need to keep calm and be

The 'sit' whistle can be introduced when walking the dog on the lead. Initially it is preceded with a verbal command.

consistent.

Once you are confident that your dog fully understands what the sit whistle means and is responding to it without the verbal backup, now is the time you can begin to develop this a bit further. However, do not overdo this exercise as you can end up making the dog a bit sticky and it can start to anticipate the game. When the dog is hunting about on the grass and is not looking at you, pip your whistle and if you have done your foundation work the dog will spin round and sit. Immediately throw out a retrieve as a reward. You may be surprised how quickly a young dog connects the whistle, sit and a reward. Ideally you should have done your steadying work before undertaking this exercise, so the dog doesn't run into the retrieve. If your dog isn't completely steady, then delay the time before throwing the dummy and make sure the dog has responded to the whistle command and is sitting.

It is always harder to try and stop a dog when it is coming back towards you. Inevitably you blow the whistle and the dog takes a few steps before deciding to stop, and this is where your consistency plays a major role. Sit the dog up in front of you at distance and recall it in, blow your stop whistle and as you do step forward to the dog. You have to balance the speed of the dog and its reactions; they do not have disc brakes and if they are travelling at speed, it will take a few steps to come to a halt, but you have to decide whether they are pushing their luck, or it is just their momentum. You need to be consistent when training this exercise. If the dog moves on after you blow your whistle there has to be a consequence and the normal course of action would be to go out to the dog, collect it up and put it back on the exact spot when you blew the whistle. Do not accept the dog moving, be sharp with your command, do not blow long drawn-out whistles as this can lead to long drawn-out stops, sharp is ... sharp does!

There is a gundog term that experienced handlers know only too well and that is 'going off the whistle' and that can particularly apply to the stop/ sit whistle. There are a few ways you can sharpen things up – however these will not work unless you have done the initial foundation training exercises. Once the dog has some experience, is hunting heavier cover and is steady to thrown dummies a good way to sharpen up a sloppy stop is to get the dog hunting. Blow the command and immediately throw out a ball or dummy. By doing this you are in fact simulating a flush. The dog should not at this stage run in on the retrieve; you are re-establishing the connection between the stop whistle and something good happening, i.e. the dummy being thrown.

This is another play on a previous exercise, but we are looking for a more dynamic reaction from the dog. Either sit the dog up in front of you or recall it whilst hunting and as it is moving towards you blow the whistle and throw out a dummy or ball. If need be you can again step in towards the dog just to reinforce your command. Depending on the dog's reaction it can have the retrieve or go and pick it up yourself. Again, don't overdo this exercise as it can make the dog sticky on the recall, but it is a good way of reminding the dog of the connections of whistle, sit, retrieve and staying steady.

Another really effective exercise to help give the dog confidence when stopping at a distance is to sit the dog and throw out a dummy behind it. Obviously the dog has to be steady. Walk away from the dog and stop when

Using a retrieve as a reward for responding to the sit whistle can quickly progress the lesson.

you are about 20 metres apart. When you are ready call the dog in towards you and at around halfway blow your stop command. You should get a sharp response from the dog as it will still be concentrating on the dummy and when it hears the stop whistle it will be thinking that you will send it back for the retrieve. Gradually you can extend the distance that you move back from the dog. Be careful that you don't get into a habit of giving the command at around the same distance each time and occasionally when the dog has stopped walk back and pick up the dummy yourself: keep the dog guessing.

A poor recall is something that can quite often develop as a young pup reaches adolescence. When you first bring home your eight-week-old puppy it will basically want to be with you and around you. You are the centre of its world. If it has been bred properly it will have had plenty of human contact and so it will naturally have learnt that all good things, especially food, come from its breeder and now its new owner. During the early stages of puppyhood most owners will spend plenty of time interacting with their new pup, teaching them the basics such as sit, wait and, of course, to come when called and quite often a ready supply of treats will encourage the pup to respond to their new lessons. As the pup starts to get older and begins to realise that there is a big wide world outside its home and there are lots of exciting smells to explore, the human and treats start to become less interesting and then at around seven to eight months your sweet little pup turns into a Teenage Mutant Ninja adolescent nightmare!

When stopping the dog on a recall, take a few steps towards the dog at the same time you blow the 'sit' whistle and make sure you are giving a clear hand signal.

Two things happen. The first is that the dog's hormones are developing and just like teenage kids they begin to think they know it all. They want to stretch as many boundaries as they can get away with. The second is that their noses kick in, and this most highly developed instrument will lead the dog to more exciting things and, before you know it, the dog is off over the horizon and is totally deaf to your desperate calls for it to come back. Working on recall is something you will be constantly developing even with older trained dogs; you will have to repeatedly go back to some basic exercises to remind them of what is required.

If you have used the place board you will have already used the rapid pip of the recall whistle to get the dog to come and sit on the board. Once again you are teaching the dog the recall without it really even knowing it but there are plenty of other ways to instil a solid recall whistle. This is one exercise, where in the early stages a food treat can really benefit the dog's training and can produce very quick results. Initially you will be using a verbal command such as 'here' or 'come', and once you have settled on what word you are going to use, be consistent with it. Each time the dog comes back to you give it a food reward. Remember in most cases when you call the dog you will be asking it to break away from doing something interesting, so your reward has to be of higher value. A piece of liver sausage is a higher value than a piece of the dog's kibble. Once the dog is consistently coming back to your verbal command you can then add in a few rapid pips on your whistle when it is on the way back. Once again it's that association training coming into play. At this a stage you can also introduce a physical cue and that is to open both your arms at the side of your body as though you are inviting the dog to come back to you.

You can, of course, set up a more formal way of teaching the recall whistle by sitting the dog up in front of you at a distance and verbally calling it into you whilst using your whistle. The connection will once again

Some dogs lack confidence when being asked to sit at a distance and will creep forward. Setting out a retrieve behind the dog can help to overcome this issue.

develop. Just a cautious word of warning: this method can cause your dog to become unsteady on its stays, so every now and again do walk back to the dog, so it doesn't begin second-guessing what is going to happen. Another opportunity to teach the recall whistle is when the dog is coming back to you with a retrieve. If you have done your foundation work properly your dog should go out and pick a dummy or ball and come straight back to you. All you have to do is give the recall whistle command when the dog is heading back to you. These subtle methods can work really well once you have established the behaviour, especially using a high-value food reward in the early stages of training.

The turn whistle is predominantly used when hunting your gundog. It is basically a shortened version of the recall whistle. When hunting your dog and developing a quartering pattern (see the Hunting chapter) each time you change direction you give a couple of short pips on the whistle. The dog will see your body moving in the opposite direction and will turn and come across you. It will hear the associated whistle command and over time it will connect the two actions together.

Getting your gundog to hold or hunt a specific area after being sent out for a retrieve is an important skill for a number of reasons. The first and the most obvious is that if your dog has not marked a shot bird but you have been given a mark by a Gun or indeed you have seen the bird fall, you can get the dog out to the rough area and then give it a whistle command so that it will get its nose down and sweep that specific area. Another factor to bear in mind is that if you can get your dog out to an area and hold it there rather than it running all over the place, it is less likely that other game will be disturbed potentially spoiling the day's shooting. There are no hard and fast rules as to when you can start to train a dog to hold a specific area, and you certainly should not put an age target on the dog. Each one will be different and progress at a different pace. However, as with all gundog training the dog needs to have learnt a series of exercises if you are to prevent problems in the future. These must be fully ingrained in the dog before you move on to the next task. In the case of training a dog to hold an area the dog must be a sound and reliable retriever on seen, blind and memory retrieves, have a solid stop whistle and be steady to thrown retrieves.

There are several techniques you can employ to train a dog to get its nose down and hunt a particular area. Depending on the dog's ability and confidence you can use one or more of each of the methods. Each and every dog is different, and it is important to be able to assess your dog and adjust your training as needed. One of the easiest ways of getting a young gundog of any breed to get its nose down and start to hunt an area is, in fact, by using some very small dummies and an area of rough grass. It is important that you use the same area for all the initial training sessions as this will help to build up the dog's confidence.

Start by letting the dog see that you have a small dummy in your hand and then sit the dog next to you and simply throw the dummy into the rough grass. To start with send the dog quite quickly but after a couple of sessions turn the dog away and walk the dog off for a few feet just so that it loses the exact area where the dummy landed. The next step is the all-important part of the exercise. You need to introduce a command that the dog will associate with putting its nose down and finding the reward. Like all whistle commands there has to be a precursor verbal command, and, in this case, there are three distinct types of command that can be used, either on their own or as a combination – verbal, whistle and hand – and which one(s) you use will depend mainly on the distance the dog is working away from you. Whichever command you decide to use, timing is all important. When you are ready send the dog towards the area that you threw the dummy, initially keep the distance quite short and as soon as you see the dog's nose go down introduce your command.

If you have developed a strong retrieving instinct in your gundog, you can simply introduce the recall whistle as it comes back to you.

There are numerous verbal commands that are used in gundog training to hold a dog in an area or to ask it to hunt for a retrieve. The most common one is 'hi lost', and you may have also heard a handler use 'there ... there'. To be honest it really doesn't matter what word you use; it is the connection with the dog's action that is important. Basically, you say the command, the dog finds the dummy and the dog will quickly associate your words with finding something and the connection is made. When the dog is eventually working at a distance from you, especially in the case of the retrieving breeds, it is easier and more effective to use a simple whistle command. Most handlers when introducing the hunt whistle use a long and then a short peep: 'Peeeeeep ... peeep ... peeeeeep ... peeep'. Initially you use both a verbal and the whistle command until the dog fully understands what the combination of the two commands mean.

When using the rapid pips of the recall whistle you can also introduce an open arms physical cue to encourage the dog.

Dogs have far more effective eyesight than humans with regard to movement and therefore a physical signal can also be used to great effect, especially in conditions where the dog is having difficulty in hearing a verbal command due to high winds or fast-flowing streams. You can always back up either your verbal or whistle command with a hand signal. When the dog has its nose down hold your hand at waist height and move your hand slowly from side to side. You are almost mimicking the way the dog is working the ground. At this stage, the dog is right under your nose, and it may seem a bit pointless but as the distance between you and the dog is increased this signal will become more relevant.

Ideally for this next exercise you need a willing helper. You will also need a point of reference: an electric fencing stake is ideal and easily carted around with a couple of dummies or tennis balls. First of all, walk your dog out to the stake and show it the dummy as you throw it on the ground, turn the dog and walk away. Keep the stake to your back and throw out a long-seen retrieve. You are going to send the dog for this retrieve first. If you are on your own whilst the dog is running out to the dummy, quickly go back and pick up the retrieve by the stake, put it away and go and take the seen retrieve from the dog. If you have a helper, simply get them to pick it up and get them to move away from the spot.

Once you have the seen retrieve to hand, turn the dog and send him for the retrieve that he thinks is in the area around the stake. The next step is very important. As the dog gets to the area by the stake you must stop it on the whistle and if you have trained it right, the dog should stop and look at you for the next command. This is when you use your combination of verbal, whistle, and physical signals to start the dog hunting. The reason you have removed the dummy is so that if the dog does ignore your command or in fact finds the dummy straight away, you won't have the chance to put the process of send out, stop, look at me, signal, hunt ... and that ultimately is the point of the whole exercise. Let the dog hunt the area using plenty of encouragement by way of your chosen command. If you have a helper, when the dog isn't looking get them to drop the retrieve back into the area or if you are on your own you will have to try to sneak it back in without the dog seeing it. It is important that at this stage the dog has constant success so it is conditioned to believe that every time it hears or sees the combination of signals, if it gets his nose down the dog will find something. Over time you can gradually increase the distance and difficulty of the retrieves to the point where you are putting blinds out at a long distance for the dog to find.

The turn whistle is introduced when hunting your gundog and will correspond with you turning your body.

To begin teaching a dog to hold and hunt an area a combination of whistle, verbal and physical cues can be used.

# 9. Steadiness

CATO
OUTDOORS
WWW.CATOOUTDOORS.COM

In the initial stages of your gundog's training, you will have been developing the drive and desire of the dog. You have been conditioning it to be a really keen retriever; you will have been encouraging it to get about and enjoy hunting; but at some point, you will need to begin the steadying process. In the shooting field a steady dog is a joy to spend time with; a dog that is not steady can be a nightmare. Unless you are completely new to the gundog world, on a shoot day you will have no doubt seen various breeds of gundogs chasing birds and ground game, and you may have also witnessed so-called peg dogs being tied to a stake and doing a pretty good impression of a kite on a windy day. An unsteady dog really can ruin your day.

Throughout a gundog's life there will be conflicts in its training. You will teach it to hunt and perhaps flush game, but you will not want the dog to chase it. On the other hand, if they find and have a flush and you end up with a runner you will then want the dog to run after the quarry and bring it back to you. It can be confusing enough for the handler to get their head around this let alone the dog. Dogs learn by repetition, whether that is good behaviour or bad behaviour, and that is basically how a verbal command works. The handler uses a phrase and the dog learns the behaviour that corresponds to that verbal instruction. Over time you repeat that command, and the dog learns to connect the two aspects together. There are some commands that you will teach your gundog that can be taught from an early age and will stay with it for the remainder of the dog's working career. 'Sit', 'stay', 'heel', 'come' are just a few of the more common ones but the 'leave it' command is the one that if you can condition your dog to understand it right from the beginning will make your training far easier going forward. If you have followed the place board exercises you will see how useful the board is to begin the steadying process but if you have bypassed that aspect of the dog's training, you can still go through the process, but it may be a bit more challenging.

The 'leave it' command is important for a number of reasons, but it really becomes important when you start more advanced training such as leaving the area of a contact flush or when you need to redirect the dog from one retrieve to another. Think of it as a switch off command. That basically means the dog needs to switch off from what it is currently doing and refocus on something else. That something else maybe you or another task. Consistency is the key in training this command. When you give the command, the dog must obey each and every time and you want to get to the point where the dog reacts immediately to the instruction. If you allow the dog to be sloppy in his reaction this may well cause you issues in the later stages of his training. The earlier you start getting your gundog used to the

In the shooting field a steady dog is a joy to spend time with ...

'leave it' command the better and this can be introduced even as a young pup. Remember this is an all-encompassing command and as with all things related to gundog training you gradually build up the training and in turn you also increase the temptation for the dog.

Always turn in to the dog so you are blocking the dog from the retrieve. This will prevent the dog from lunging at the dummy.

You can start to introduce the 'leave it' command quite early on, and feed time can be a good opportunity to do this. The dog will already be used to sitting before you give its food so as you put the bowl down, give the command. If the dog moves forward, which it will do in the early stages quickly lift the bowl and start again. Most young dogs get the idea quite quickly. Once the dog has grasped the exercise, leave it sitting for a bit longer before letting it eat. Look to take all opportunities to condition your gundog to certain commands. When they are out and about in the garden is another good time to bring the 'leave it' command into play. When the dog is occupied, perhaps sniffing something, call its name and then add the 'leave it' command. You may have to crouch down to really encourage the dog to come to you and make sure you give it plenty of praise. It is learning the exercise by default and eventually you should be able to just use the 'leave it' command, and the dog should leave what it is doing and come straight to you. Remember, repetition is the key.

This next stage should not be done until you are confident that you have instilled a solid retrieving desire in your dog as the process can sometimes initially reduce the drive to go and pick up a retrieve. Also the dog should have a good sit/stay. At this stage, your dog should be quite used to the command 'leave it' in their everyday life so this process will hopefully be a fairly straightforward progression. Keep the dog on a lead and throw out a dummy. Up until now the dog will be used to running straight in for the retrieve. Tap your leg and walk away using the 'leave it' command. Always turn the dog away from the retrieve so you are between the dog and the dummy. You will probably need a few sessions of this before the dog really gets the hang of it, but there is no doubt the early conditioning of the pup will make this an easier lesson. Sit the dog and go out and pick up the dummy yourself. From now on you will be picking up most of the retrieves – the dog has to now learn that not every retrieve will be for them.

The next stage is to sit the dog and stand out in front of it and take a few steps back, give your 'leave it' command and at the same time drop a dummy just to one side. If your dog does make a dive for the retrieve, you are in a position to block it. If by some chance it does get the dummy, then you must not chastise it but take it as a retrieve and set up the exercise again, but this time be ready for the dog to run in. Gradually build this exercise up to the point where you can throw a selection of retrieves around the dog whilst it remains in place. As well as using dummies, rolling tennis or fur balls around the dog can be very tempting. When you feel that the dog is ready you can really test it. At some point you have to undertake what is known as proofing the exercise. This simply means you have to assess the dog to make sure it has fully learnt the lesson you have been teaching it. You do not want to be doing this too soon as you should never set the dog up to fail, but once you are confident you can set about assessing the dog. Whilst the dog is sitting down throw a retrieve over the top of the dog's head. You will often find that the dog will spin around to watch the dummy and if your foundation work is not in place, you may well find that the movement of the dog turning will make the dog break and run in. If this happens simply take the retrieve and next time stand closer to the dog so you can intervene if the same thing happens. Another option is to get a helper to stand next to the dummy and if the dog breaks, they can either pick it up or at the least stand on it, so the dog doesn't self-reward. Remember, each time you throw a dummy you use the 'leave it' command.

As you pick up the dummy always watch your dog and extend your free had to remind the dog to remain steady.

A dummy thrown over the dog's head will really test its steadiness. Do not rush to this stage.

Initially this may seem a repeat exercise of the standard steadiness to dummy exercise, but the significant difference is the dog will be moving when the dummy is thrown. You can do this in two ways. The first is to sit the dog at a distance from you and recall it. Halfway towards you blow the stop/sit whistle and throw out a dummy. The second way is to hunt the dog in front of you, blow the stop whistle and throw out the dummy. Initially throw the dummy between you and the dog and be prepared to block the dog should it run in, as the lesson is learnt you can then increase the temptation by throwing the dummy in front of the dog or even over its head. In the early stages make sure the dog sits. Some dogs especially cockers prefer to stop and stand.

When training a gundog in the later stages of its education you should start to try and think of exercises that correspond with potential situations you may come across in the shooting field and one of these is that the dog must be steady to any distractions, especially when out on a retrieve. Many handlers will have witnessed, or indeed experienced, the situation where a dog has been sent out for a bird and another lands or gets shot when the dog is on the way back and it drops its retrieve and heads off uncontrollably for the distraction. You can and in fact should train to avoid this happening. Not only is it embarrassing for the handler it is also not good for the swift and efficient collection of shot game, which should be the overall priority for anyone picking up or shooting over their dog.

Like all aspects of training, you must ensure that the basics are in place before moving on to this kind of exercise. If your dog is not steady, is a reluctant or poor retriever you could potentially cause further problems and matters can quickly spiral out of control. This type of exercise is more

Use a high-contrast dummy set down next to you as a distraction whilst the dog is coming back with a retrieve.

advanced and therefore the dog needs to be mentally mature enough to deal with the pressure of this particular exercise. Another thing to consider is the personality of your dog as you will be giving quite firm commands during this task. If your dog is of a sensitive nature you may have to break the exercise down and not push the dog too quickly; gauge what is going on and be prepared to adjust your training accordingly. Gradually build up each stage of the exercise and do not rush on to the next step until you are confident the dog fully understands what is required. If you find that the dog breaks and goes for the distraction dummy, try and stop it before it gets to it and self-rewards. Once the dog has the dummy in its mouth you must stay calm and take it as per a normal retrieve and then try again or go back a step in the exercise. This steadiness exercise needs to be gradually built up in steps. Make it straightforward to start with and gradually increase the temptation. At this stage we will only be using thrown dummies.

Going back to the science of a dog's vision, with this exercise we want to make the distraction as visual as possible so use high-contrast dummies as the distraction: black and white dummies work really well as do blue and white ones. Set the distraction up on the opposite side of where you will

An advanced exercise is to throw a dummy over the dog's head when it is returning with a retrieve. Just watch it doesn't drop the retrieve and go for the distraction.

position the dog – this would normally be on your right as the dog will normally be sitting on your left. Stand the dummy on its end approximately 3 metres away, not too close as to be too tempting, but not too far away so you can block the dog should it go for it on the way back. Once you are set up throw a simple seen retrieve straight out in front and send the dog. It is unlikely the dog will take any notice of the distraction on his way out as he should be focused on the dummy that had been thrown out, but as he comes back to you the high-contrast dummy will be very visible to him, so you need to be ready. As the dog comes towards you, if he looks at the distraction just take a few steps back and give a few recall blasts on your whistle. Timing is all important. If you get it right the dog will quickly refocus on you and ignore the other dummy.

Once your dog is consistently ignoring the static distraction you can move on to increasing the temptation. Set up your dog and throw out a straightforward seen retrieve. Send your dog and when he is about 2 metres from you on the way back throw out another dummy to one side and slightly behind you. Do not watch where the dummy goes – keep your eyes on the dog and reinforce the recall command as you throw the distraction. Be prepared to block the dog should he try and run past you to the distraction. It can be a bit easier if you have someone to help and they can throw the distraction, and you can solely concentrate on the dog. The next stage can really test the dog. Set up a simple seen retrieve as per the previous exercise but this time as the dog is coming back to you throw a dummy directly over the top of the dog's head. Again, be ready to enforce the recall whistle. It is fine for the dog to watch the distraction and mark it down; it doesn't even matter if it stops and watches it land but be on your guard that it doesn't drop the dummy it is carrying to go out after the distraction.

As has been mentioned gundog training is about gradually building up the dog's confidence and understanding of what will be required in the

A gundog should not only be steady to the 'flush' but also to the sound of shot. This is the combination of events that will happen in the shooting field.

shooting field. In basic terms each individual step of the dog's training will at some point connect in with other aspects and hopefully create a complete picture for both dog and handler. From the early stages of the dog's education, you will have begun by getting the dog used to the 'sit' command. This will have been started by using a verbal cue 'sit' and then a whistle command, a single blast. You will then have moved on to having the dog sitting in front of you and thrown dummies around him, teaching the dog to be steady and to ignore the retrieves. If these parts of your training are fully understood and embedded in your dog it is time to move on and begin the process of connecting some other pieces of the gundog training puzzle.

In the shooting field a gundog should basically stop or sit to three situations: the whistle, the flush of ground or feathered game, and it should also stop to shot. In most practical cases the handler will be giving a blast on the stop whistle just as game flushes. Obviously a shot will follow but there are what can be considered refinements. A very well-trained dog will stop to a flush or shot without any intervention from the handler, and this can come in useful if the dog is hunting in heavy cover and flushes game without the handler being able to see it. A dog that will stop to shot and acknowledges the shot, looks in the direction of the sound, is worth its weight in gold especially if you are shooting with other Guns and your dog may be required to make a retrieve from one of your fellow Guns.

The next step is to get the dog to stop and be steady to an artificial flush and the shot from a starting pistol. As has already been implied, training your gundog to stop to a flush and/or shot is undertaken in steps and you cannot even begin this process if your dog will not sit at a distance from you, is not steady to thrown dummies and is not on the stop whistle. These three lessons are the foundation blocks that will allow you to progress. The progression to 'stopping or being steady to shot' is simply another step on from the previous exercises, which should be fully learnt and understood by the dog before moving on. Hunt or recall the dog and when it is moving blow the stop whistle, throw the dummy and fire the shot. Because the dog has already learnt to stop to the whistle and a thrown dummy, the shot is just another layer in the exercise. Take things slowly as there is a lot to think about and make sure you follow the sequence. Again be prepared to block the dog from running in on the retrieve as the shot will add a bit of excitement to the exercise. To add further temptation to this exercise you can eventually replace the dummy with some cold game, but as this really ups the excitement don't move on too quickly.

When you are confident that the dog has grasped the concept of the lesson you can test or 'proof' the exercise. This time you will not be using

If you plan to shoot over your gundog, it is imperative it is steady to the flush of game to enable a safe shot.

the stop whistle; you will be depending on the dog stopping to just a thrown dummy and/or the starting pistol shot. Set the dog up exactly as you have in previous exercises and this time when the dog is moving either throw the dummy OR fire a shot. Obviously you will have to try both. If the dog doesn't stop, you will have to go back to using the whistle and reinforce the original lesson.

At some point you will have to move on from steadiness on dummies to live game. Once again a rabbit or steadying pen can really pay dividends, but even if you don't have access to a pen with birds or rabbits in you could still use a local town centre where there are a few feral pigeons or a park with a pond that has a few ducks paddling about to further this part of the dog's training. By now your dog should know exactly what 'leave it' means although at each stage as you up the temptation you should be prepared to take a step back. Begin by walking the dog around the bird pen on the lead and each time it shows too much interest give a sharp 'leave it' and turn and walk in the opposite direction. You could do exactly the same thing with the feral pigeons in a town centre or the ducks on a local pond. Sometimes you just have to think outside the box. You want to get to the stage where you can sit the dog up in a pen or at the side of a pond and be confident that the dog understands that 'leave it' means leave it.

Earlier in the dog's training you may have used a rabbit pen to develop the young dog's hunting drive and you have now steadied the dog to thrown dummies. By now it should also be on the stop whistle, and it is time to put the brakes on the dog and steady them to the flush of feathered game or rabbit. Some handlers do not consider this a necessary part of a young gundog's training and are quite happy for the dog to move on after a flush provided it doesn't give chase. However, if you plan to compete in working tests or field trials or even just shoot over your dog, then it really must stop when it flushes game. There are a number of reasons for this. First of all there is the safety factor – if you are shooting over your dog you want to be able to get a clear shot without any fear of hitting the dog. The second is that if the dog starts chasing, not only do you risk the chance of losing it, but the dog will also be disturbing the ground and flushing more game and chasing it, so you can see how very quickly things can get out of control.

Ideally, if you can get access to a rabbit pen then the process of getting the dog steady to the flush can be set up and therefore will be easier to control. The most important thing with this training exercise is that you as the handler must have your wits about you and be ready to act. It helps if the cover in the pen is not too thick as you want the dog to see the rabbit run or pheasant flush. Work the dog up the pen, preferably with the wind blowing directly towards the dog, keep the quartering pattern tight and the dog fairly close to you, make sure you have your whistle in your mouth as you will need to be really sharp with the stop whistle.

By now you should be able to read your dog's body language and should be able to recognise when it has winded something. As soon as the dog makes the flush give a short sharp blast on the whistle and as you should be quite close to the dog just take a quick step forward to reinforce the fact you want the dog to sit. If your foundation work has been done properly the dog should respond immediately. If the dog moves, catch it and place it back on the spot of the flush and give it a few blows of the whistle and the 'sit' command, wait a minute or so, and then repeat the exercise. Once you have had a couple of flushes, stop for the day as you don't want to overdo things as this can make the dog a bit sticky with its hunting until the lesson gets fully understood.

Another really useful method of teaching a dog to stop to the flush of feathered game is to use homing pigeons. It is appreciated that not everyone has access to these, but most professional trainers will keep a loft with a few birds in and to be honest it is well worth paying for a few lessons when you get to this stage of the dog's training. There are a number of ways that pigeons can be used in getting a dog steady. The first is that the bird is flipped out in front of the dog when it is hunting. The handler must really concentrate, because as soon as the bird flies off you must be ready to blow the stop whistle and be ready to stop the dog from chasing. It can take few goes but

Be ready to react should your gundog's body language change. It could indicate a flush is imminent.

Hunting your dog in the corner of a rabbit pen will enable you to keep a level of control on the dog should it make a find.

most dogs get the idea relatively quickly. The second way is to use what is known as a bird launcher. This is a remote-control piece of equipment where a bird is placed in a spring-loaded hammock and when the dog indicates the bird, the bird is released and is launched upwards and flies away. These are normally used in the training of the hunt, point, retrieve breeds and although they can be effective, they are quite noisy and can scare a sensitive dog.

The third method is to 'dizzy' the pigeon. This does need some level of skill as if it is done too much the bird will be reluctant to flush and may get pegged (caught) by the dogs and that is not desirable. It is highly recommended that you seek the advice of an experienced and professional gundog trainer who can ensure that both you and your dog are ready to take this step.

There are plenty of gizmos and gadgets on the market that can really help with your gundog training, especially steadiness training. But like everything they should be used in moderation, and you need to think about what you are aiming to achieve when setting up an exercise. Additionally there may be legal implications to consider before parting with your hard-earned cash. Legally, you cannot fire a blank-firing dummy launcher in a public place and therefore you will need to have access to private ground to be able to use one, so unless you have permission and somewhere you can use one, save your money and look for an alternative.

One of the most common questions that is asked by novice trainers is, 'When can I use a dummy launcher?' It seems that everyone wants to start launching dummies long distances with loud bangs well before their dogs are ready and without really understanding not only the benefits of the tool but also the negative aspects. As with any piece of gundog training equipment you need to think not only how you use it but also why you want to use it. Yes, it can be that using a launcher is exciting and it can make the novice feel like a 'proper' trainer but used wrongly and at the wrong time in the dog's training you stand a good chance of at the very least scaring the dog and, worse, creating behaviours that will be extremely difficult to overcome in the future.

The main use of a dummy launcher is to train the dog to mark at a distance and to associate the sound of a bang with a retrieve, and therein lies the problem. If you go back to your early steadiness training when you sat your dog and threw dummies and balls all around it, the rule was that you would go and pick nine out of every ten yourself and perhaps let the dog have the odd retrieve. This was all about not letting the dog think that every retrieve was for it. Bring in a dummy launcher that is going to shoot a dummy over a distance of 75 metres and without fail the handler will be sending the dog for every retrieve, because we are lazy and don't want to walk that distance to pick it ourselves. The dog will very quickly realise that every time it hears a bang it will get a retrieve and, in no time at all, you have a dog that is running in as soon as you fire the launcher, and you have another problem that you have to go and sort out.

You shouldn't even contemplate introducing your dog to a dummy

Homing pigeons can be a really effective way of steadying a gundog to the flush of game.

launcher until it has heard the sound of a starting pistol and is confident with that scenario. Starting pistols use .22 short blanks which are quite loud and totally different to a shotgun being fired. A dummy launcher uses .22 long blanks and is substantially louder than a starting pistol. A word of caution: never fire a launcher without a dummy attached as the crack of the blank is enough to unnerve even the most experienced of dogs. Assuming you have all your basic training in place and your dog is mature enough and ready for this step you can consider introducing the launcher. Ideally you would want someone else to fire it so you can concentrate on the dog and make sure it is not only okay with the bang but also it is not going to run into the fall of the dummy.

As mentioned earlier most dummy launchers use .22 long blanks and these come in three strengths: green (lowest), yellow (medium) and red (high). Generally, the green or yellow blanks are sufficient. The yellow strength will propel a dummy around 50 to 75 metres, and this is quite far enough for most training needs. They also have the power to push a rubber dummy over and through even rough grass. More importantly you will be able to deal with the recoil easier than using the high-power red blanks.

Believe it or not there is a right and a wrong way to hold a handheld dummy launcher and if you get it wrong it will hurt. Even so-called low recoil handheld launchers will still kick. If you hold the launcher straight armed with your thumb at the firing mechanism end the recoil will travel straight down your wrist into your arm and there is nothing to absorb the pressure. The right way is to turn your hand so your thumb is at the back of the launcher and your arm is bent and this will help to create a shock absorber and, therefore, significantly reduce the recoil. A preferred option is to use a shoulder-mounted unit. This turns it into a gun-like launcher. This not only helps to absorb more pressure and recoil, it is also a great way of simulating a walk-up shoot especially when training spaniels. Add a rubber dummy and you have the perfect tool for laying shot lines along the ground. There are a few variations on the market. With some you simply add an extension onto a handheld launcher, but make sure you check your model for compatibility first. Others are purpose built and can be a better option although they may be a bit more expensive especially if you already have a handheld launcher that can be adapted.

Remote-controlled launchers have become very popular over the past few years and the biggest advantage of these is that if you train on your own you can fire the dummy away from your position and this teaches the dog to look forward and to not always expect a retrieve to come from the handler. You can buy some quite sophisticated remote launchers that have up to eight individual launcher tubes that can be fired at any angle and rotation and can also be fitted with a sound box to simulate the sound of game birds flushing. Another option that is available and can be very useful if you are in a situation where you can't use a blank-firing launcher is a remote air launcher. Instead of a .22 blank they use compressed air that is forced up through a tube to launch the dummy. These units do not make such a loud noise, which can be useful if you have a sensitive dog or are in a situation where there are houses nearby. You may find that the dummies will not travel so far and as they tend to be lighter, they can also be affected by the wind. This can reduce the distance they will travel although this can be offset by the fact that the units tend to be remotely fired so the distance from the dog can be increased simply by moving the launcher further away. The air compressor models are quieter and can basically be used anywhere and although they do not have the 'shot sound' this can be introduced by using a starting pistol to shoot at the dummy as it is launched. Depending on the release system most remote launchers can be fired a considerable distance from the operator, so they can give you plenty of training scenario options. However, they are obviously more expensive than a handheld type.

There are several different kinds of launcher dummies available, and they do have distinct characteristics when fired. The normal long dummies are the most common and depending on which power of blanks you use will go an average distance. If you use a dummy with streamers attached, these can help the dog to mark although this kind tend not to go quite so far as the streamers create more air resistance and, therefore, you may need to use a higher-powered blank. The hard rubber ball or torpedo-shaped dummies go the furthest and are really good for laying a scent line along the ground to simulate a shot rabbit.

Holding a dummy launcher this way will cause the recoil to travel up the handler's arm, which can be quite uncomfortable.

The correct way to hold a dummy launcher that will allow the handler's arm to act as a shock absorber.

The importance of using any kind of dummy launcher carefully has to be emphasised, and with thought they can be a really useful tool. But if not used sparingly you may undo a lot of your initial steadiness work and will find that you have inadvertently encouraged your dog to run in ... you have been warned!

Not everyone has the luxury of being able to use a rabbit or steadying pen so you may have to look at alternatives. Ground game such as rabbits or hares can be the undoing of the steadiest of gundogs and even if you live in an area where it is unlikely that you will come across these furry creatures, you should still train your dog to be steady to the bolting of this kind of quarry. Bolting rabbit set-ups take two forms, basic and advanced, and as you can probably guess one is more expensive than the other. You would introduce these simulations in exactly the same way you would use the rabbit pen.

The basic type of bolting rabbit is made up of a long piece of heavy-duty elastic. One end has a stake to enable it to be fixed into the ground and the other end has a fur-covered dummy attached. You will also have some kind of manual quick-release clip. The idea is that you stretch the elastic and fasten the dummy to the release clip. You then work your dog up towards the dummy and just as the dog winds or gets to the dummy you pull the release, and the dummy shoots out to simulate the flush of a rabbit. Although this can work okay there are some distinct disadvantages. First of all, the flush is really short as you will only be able to stretch the elastic so far. It also makes quite a noise which can frighten a sensitive dog. Additionally, timing has to be nigh on perfect as you do not want to hit the dog with a fast-moving dummy.

Compressed air remote dummy launchers have fewer legal restrictions on them and can be a bit quieter to operate.

The remote RRT Versa Launcher uses .22 long blanks and has the unique ability that each individual tube can be positioned at any angle or rotation.

Another option is a remote lure machine. These have been traditionally used for lurcher or whippet racing and for training birds of prey, but they are also an excellent tool for teaching a gundog to be steady to fur. A rabbit skin is attached to a line that runs back to a motorised reel. When the remote is pressed the reel spins and pulls the line and lure. Some models even have variable speeds which can be really useful depending on the exercise that you are setting up. You can also purchase roller wheels that you can stick in the ground to vary the direction that the lure flushes and with a bit of thought you can get a number of flushes during one hunt with the dog. Obviously, these units are far more expensive but using one can really take your training to another level and the biggest advantage is that you can set them up anywhere. One day you could train on a rough grass field and then the next day take it to some woodland and the next into some cover crop: the options are endless.

As well as using a rabbit lure for steadying you can also incorporate it into your distraction exercises. Sit your dog with the lure set up so it will run across in front of the dog left to right. There is a good reason for setting it up like this. Throw out a seen retrieve and when you are ready, flush the lure. You will now have to be ready as when you send the dog for the seen retrieve you do not want it to go for the lure and this is why you set the distraction to run from left to right, so you are in a better position to block the dog. A variation on the above is to set up the exercise in the same way but this time you send the dog for the retrieve and flush the lure when the dog is on the way back. This time you need to be ready with a strong recall command as the lure flushes in front of the dog. These exercises all have practical applications in the shooting field as quite often a dog will move unshot game when out on a retrieve and you don't want it to be distracted from the job you have asked it to do.

There is an old saying in the gundog world and that is 'The dog you have in January isn't the same dog you had in September.' Basically, that time period is the majority of the game shooting season. At the beginning of the season your dog will be on the money; by the end of the season the chances are it could be bordering on being feral and after perhaps hundreds of flushes and hearing the stop whistle numerous times the dog's steadiness will almost certainly have deteriorated. So, this aspect of the dog's training is something that you will no doubt have to constantly revisit throughout the dog's working life.

# 10. Introduction to Shot

Acclimatising your gundog to shot is something that should be carefully planned and not rushed.

The introduction to shot or more correctly to the sound of shot is part of a gundog's training that should not be taken lightly and needs careful planning. Fortunately, through selective breeding 'gun shyness' is something that is not often see in gundogs today. However, although genetically it is less likely to occur it can be brought on by poor or indeed ill-informed training. It is not something to be rushed into. Many novice owners are keen to see if their young dogs will be all right with the sound of gunshot as they are worried about putting in a lot of effort and training only to find that their hope for the future is scared of loud bangs. On the subject of loud bangs, there is a difference between the sound of a gun and a firework and it's not unusual for a gundog to be perfectly okay with a shotgun being fired but really not happy about the loud bangs on Fireworks Night.

Another question that is often asked is whether taking a young dog to a clay shooting ground is a good idea. This is not a good idea for a number of reasons. The first is the amount and volume of sound: most clay grounds have sound bunds or banks to contain the noise, and this creates an echo which can be very unnerving for a dog. The sound can also be pretty constant and more importantly there is nothing positive for the dog to connect to the sound. Problems can quickly develop. Imagine this scenario: the dog starts to show signs of concern and perhaps even begins to whine. The handler's natural response is to try and calm the dog by giving it attention and perhaps even indirectly praising it: 'Good boy ... it's okay.' It is not a big step for the dog to connect his behaviour with the reaction of his owner and before you know it you will have a dog that may develop anxiety and start making a noise.

It can be expected that any gundog will be exposed to the sound of shot, although this can be in different ways. If you plan to go beating with your dog, in most cases the sound will be in the distance and is unlikely to cause any issues for the dog. On the other hand, if you plan to shoot over your dog, either on a peg, in a hide or walked-up/rough shooting, the noise can be very close, and you will need a dog that is totally comfortable with the sound. Do not put a fixed age on introducing a dog to shot. It depends on a few factors. The first is the dog's personality and confidence level. If you have a dog with a soft nature, it is better to hold off a little bit longer than if the dog is bold and confident, but in any event, you need to get a good level of basic obedience and a high retrieving drive as you will use this when introducing shot for the first time. Before explaining the process, a few words of caution. The first is regarding what you use to make the 'bang'.

Some people may consider using a dummy launcher (without a dummy attached). However, due to the fact that a launcher uses a long .22 blank

... it's not unusual for a gundog to be perfectly okay with a shotgun being fired but really not happy about the loud bangs on Fireworks Night.

A willing helper to fire a starting pistol at a distance can be a real bonus when introducing the sound of shot to a gundog.

cartridge and there is nothing to suppress the sound, it can make an incredibly loud noise and what can be described as a 'crack' rather than a bang and this really can scare a young dog. It is suggested you invest in a proper starting pistol that uses the quieter .22 short blanks and please do not use it in a public place as you may well end up with a visit from the local police.

As already mentioned, you need to get a strong retrieving drive into your dog before introducing it to shot and you can use this desire to find a dummy to your advantage. You can begin to desensitise a young dog to loud noises by banging food bowls around them, slamming doors and generally making a bit of a row. It can be beneficial when introducing this exercise if you have a helper who can start off firing the starter pistol at a distance; however, there are some techniques that will work if you train by yourself. If the dog at any time shows signs of being concerned or worried about the noise, stop and try another day ... do not rush.

The whole principle behind this exercise is that your dog connects something positive with the sound of shot and that is a retrieve. If you have done your basic retrieving work the dog will not be thinking of anything else other than getting out to the dummy. Begin with the dog sitting next to you and throw out a dummy. You can walk the dog away for a few metres, like a memory retrieve, just to increase the desire for the retrieve. Ideally you need to have a game bag for this exercise and make sure the gun is loaded and ready. Send the dog for the dummy. When it is about halfway out, fire a shot into the bag. This helps to muffle the sound. The dog will be so focused on getting out to the retrieve it is unlikely to take any notice of the sound. Practise this a few times and constantly gauge the dog's behaviour to make sure it is comfortable with the sound of the shot.

Once you are confident that your dog is quite happy, take the gun out of the bag and repeat the exercise, but this time fire it behind your back as the dog goes out for the retrieve. The sound will obviously be louder but to a degree will be muffled by your body. The next stage is to fire the shot as the dog comes back towards you, but again initially do this when the dog is about three-quarters of the way back and build it up to the point where you are firing the shot when the dog is nearly back to you.

The final stage with the starter pistol is to repeat the steps above but this time you fire the gun out to one side. By now the dog should be quite accustomed to the sound and show no signs of distress or lack of confidence. You can then move on to building the exercises up using a shotgun (obviously DO NOT fire it into a game bag). This is a really positive way of introducing shot and provided you have done your basics properly most well-bred gundogs cope with this part of their training without any issues.

If you have developed a high retrieving instinct in your gundog you can use this to give a positive aspect to introducing shot.

# 11. Gun Sense

It is a good idea to desensitise a gundog to having something waved around above them and if you can't use a shotgun a walking stick will work just as well.

A dog that has 'gun sense' is a real attribute in the shooting field whether you are picking up, shooting over your dog, or even hunting them in a line for walking Guns. Some dogs just have natural gun sense, it seems to be in their DNA; however other dogs have to be taught the skill and it is something that you should incorporate into your dog's practical gundog training.

Before looking at how gun sense can be trained let's look at why it is so beneficial in practical terms to the handler. The easiest way to explain this is that you want the dog to learn that a possible retrieve is going to come from the direction that a gun is pointing or the sound of a shot, and it may surprise you how quickly they can catch on. A dog's eyesight is particularly sensitive to movement so the very action of you mounting a gun will draw the dog's eye to you. But ultimately, you do not want it to be looking at you – it needs to be looking at the direction the gun is pointing. Imagine your dog is unsighted from the flush but can see the handler and has learnt that when sent for the retrieve if it takes a line in the direction the gun was pointing it will find its retrieve: that is far more efficient than being handled, especially if it is a pricked bird or a legged rabbit and needs to be picked quickly.

Gun sense in a dog is not only visual – it can also be audible. If you have ever seen retrievers walking to heel in a line of walking guns, you will see how quickly the dogs acknowledge the sound of shot no matter how far up the line it is. But, if they are sent for a retrieve, they don't run to the Gun, they run out in the direction the shot was taken, which is another form of gun sense. In competition a dog that has good gun sense can make the difference between winning and losing, providing everything else is in place. Obviously, you cannot begin to train this until later in the dog's development. It should be steady to thrown dummies and have heard and be comfortable with the sound of shot.

The desensitisation of having something being swung around is something not every dog will have to undergo, but it is a process you should train just to make sure the dog is confident and is not going to be cowed by the exercise. Not everyone has the opportunity to train using a shotgun, but you can use a walking stick. Sit the dog next to and in front of you and initially simply wave the stick around the dog and watch out for any adverse reaction. At this stage you will probably find that the dog will be watching you, especially if you have developed a good eye contact. As we know, dogs learn by repetition, so the next stage is to get the dog sitting next to you and throw out a dummy and at the same time 'point' your stick in the direction of the retrieve. Your dog will inevitably look out towards the retrieve, but he will also be aware of the direction you are aiming the stick. This might sound a bit far-fetched, but it is exactly the same process as when you are training

Some dogs just have natural gun sense, it seems to be in their DNA ...

A gundog that learns the skill of following the direction that a gun is pointing will be more efficient in picking its retrieves. You can simulate this by using a stick and throwing out a dummy.

a dog to go left and right: they are following the direction you are pointing.

If you have one of the hunting breeds you will need to practise the exercise with the dog hunting out in front of you, but initially train the exercise static. Once the dog has got the idea you can move on. Set the dog off quartering and when the dog is hunting nicely throw out the dummy and again point the stick in the general direction. You can test this exercise to see if the dog understands what it needs to do by setting up a blind retrieve and pointing the stick in the direction of the dummy. In theory if the dog has fully learnt the skill, it should look in the direction you are pointing your gun.

Up until now you have been working on the visual aspect of the exercise but now you can introduce the sound of shot. This can simply be done using a starting pistol to make the bang, but you can still use a stick to simulate a shotgun. This is also where the use of a shoulder-mounted dummy launcher can really help develop the dog's gun sense. Initially, you may find the dog will again look back at you but go through the same process as above and the dog will quickly get the idea. Remember, don't always point forwards but change the angles as you would in the shooting field.

You can add further to the simulation by adding the sound of shot. A shoulder-mounted dummy launcher would work just as well.

# 12. Introducing Cold Game

Don't be too keen on getting your young gundogs on to cold game as it can put them off wanting to pick artificial retrieves.

Most if not all your early gundog training will be using tennis or fur balls and dummies, but at some point you will have to give your young dog the opportunity to pick some cold game. This can be either fur or feather but whatever you decide to use make sure it is fully defrosted and is not damaged. Ensure that there are no open wounds as this can cause all sorts of issues when asking a dog to make its first cold game retrieve. For many novice or first-time trainers this part of their dog's training can be quite nerve-racking and although for the majority of dogs it will go without any problems, as with all things, it should be done with thought and consideration.

Obviously being confident in picking up game is a vital part of a gundog's job, but it is not something that necessarily needs to be trained too early. In fact, it can have a negative effect on some dogs. It is fully understood that there is the desire for an owner to see if their dog will pick game. Introducing cold game too early however in a dog's training can put them off wanting to retrieve dummies. Cockers can be especially prone to this, and this can then make ongoing training, such as directional and handling, more challenging especially during the summer months.

Before you even consider letting your dog retrieve cold game, they should obviously be a confident and competent retriever of dummies preferably both canvas and fur. There are plenty of fur dummies available and you can now even buy cured pheasant pelts that you can tie onto normal dummies. These are a good halfway training aid, and they just get a young dog confident in picking up a retrieve that has a different texture and, of course, weight. The other consideration is that the dog must be physically able to pick up the retrieve. It is better to use small rabbits and partridges to begin with and avoid cock pheasants and duck until the dog is fully mature and strong enough to bring one back to hand. Before you even consider trying your young dog with a cold game retrieve you should ensure that they are confident in picking and delivering to hand various dummies with either pheasant pelts or wings attached to them and, of course, rabbit-fur-covered dummies. If your dog does not have a solid retrieve then you really shouldn't be moving to this next stage. A cold bird or rabbit can become real treasure for a young dog, and this can lead them to avoid coming back to the handler or even running away.

**...at some point, you will have to give your young dog the opportunity to pick some cold game.**

When setting up your initial cold game retrieves keep everything calm and try to avoid the dog getting too excited. To begin with let the dog have a few straightforward fur-covered dummy retrieves, then sit the dog up, walk out a few metres and place down your cold game. The reason that it is better to walk out and drop the game rather than throw it out is simply that this helps to keep the dog's excitement levels down. Also it is easier to set the retrieve on its breast, so it is easier for the dog to pick up.

You now have two choices when sending the dog for the retrieve: a recall pick-up or a straightforward send-out retrieve. You will need to make your decision depending on the dog's energy levels. If you have a really buzzy dog, it may be better to recall but if you have a more level-headed dog, you can send them from your side. The advantage of the recall retrieve is that

Before introducing cold game your gundog should be proficient in picking fur and feathered dummies.

the dog is coming into the cold game at a slower pace and is already coming towards you, so it just helps to reduce any excitement spikes. The first few times your dog comes across cold game it is likely that it will hesitate and be unsure of what to do and so it may need a bit of encouragement. As soon as your dog picks up the retrieve get on the recall whistle, don't give it time to think of doing anything else other than coming straight back to you, but be careful of giving the recall command too soon as you can pull the dog off the retrieve.

As with all gundog training not everything will go to plan, although in the majority of cases your gundog will take to picking up game without any issues. However, if your dog is unenthusiastic or even refuses to pick up game you will need to look at alternative methods. Despite the previous advice of keeping everything calm and maintaining low energy levels when introducing cold game, with some dogs you may need to go to the opposite end of the scale and wind them up and get them excited about the exercise. In this case don't worry about steadiness. You can go back and deal with that again once the dog has got confidence in picking up the retrieve. Take your bird and 'wave' it in front of the dog and build up the excitement levels, throw out the bird and let it run in after it. As soon as the dog shows any interest give it lots of praise and encouragement. You may have to do this a few times but normally this process works quite well and once the dog is confidently picking up the bird you can gradually go back to bringing back down the excitement levels and gaining control again.

An old-school method of introducing cold game is to put the bird inside a pair of ladies' tights. This can work really well, and as the dog gets

When setting out your cold game retrieves use small birds such as partridges or hen pheasants and place them breast-side down. This will make it easier for the dog to pick up.

A recall retrieve can be better for a really excitable dog as it takes out the speed aspect of the exercise and is far more controllable.

used to picking up the bird you then can cut a hole for the wings and the head and eventually you can remove the tights altogether. You can also buy canvas wraps that you put around the bird, and this can help with the confidence of the dog as they should already be used to picking up canvas dummies and the texture is basically the same. The one thing that your dog will have to learn for itself is to balance the cold game. Up until this point it will have probably been trained on firmer dummies and now, they will have to cope with loose wings and legs and tails dragging along the floor. There will also be weight distribution to work out and this all takes experience. This is why you shouldn't overface your dog in the early days by using cock pheasants. You can obviously build up their confidence by gradually using heavier dummies and dummies with wings and plastic heads attached in their earlier training. Gundog training isn't a case of 'one size fits all' – you will have to be adaptive according to your dog and its personality.

Wrapping cold game in a pair of ladies' tights can help to encourage a less confident dog to make the retrieve.

# 13. Obstacles

What may seem an open piece of ground to the handler can appear to be a solid block of cover from the dog's perspective.

First of all, a simple question: what is an obstacle? It doesn't necessarily have to be something solid or substantial such as a wall or a wide stream. Many dogs will find it challenging to cross over a grass ride in a wood or a ditch in a field: their natural instinct is to hit the obstacle and begin to hunt up and down it. At our eye level a group of trees or a hedge line could appear to be quite open, but the dog's perspective could be very different especially if the background is uniform. As previously mentioned, it isn't uncommon for an inexperienced dog when sent out for a retrieve to take the line and when it reaches the perceived barrier it will begin to hunt along it. Spaniels find it particularly testing to not investigate any area that may hold something of interest. You as the handler can, of course, try and handle the dog back and through the cover but it is far more efficient for the dog to plough on straight through to pick its retrieve, and you can train and teach the dog to do this.

If you are going to work your gundog in the shooting field, then having a dog than can get over an obstacle or go through rough cover to an open area to locate its retrieve in practical terms is nigh on a necessity. Depending on your location you may encounter stone walls, ditches and gullies which are covered in rushes and white grass, and quite often game, especially rabbits and pheasants which will be flushed from the rough areas and head for open ground. A gundog's natural desire is to hunt cover that it hopes will hold game and it can be the devil's own job to push the dog through and out onto open ground. It can be equally challenging to get a dog to get over a 6-foot stone wall for a retrieve that it hasn't seen ... it all takes training. Teaching and training your dog for situations you may come across in the shooting field will always stand you in good stead. Imagine you are shooting over your dog, you are hunting a hedge line, or a bank of bracken, and the dog flushes a pheasant, which gets shot and lands on the opposite side of the obstacle. Another scenario is that you are picking up and a bird gets shot out in front of you and again lands on the other side of a hedge and you need to get your dog through and out on the other side as quickly and as efficiently as possible, even more so if the bird is pricked and starts to run.

**Spaniels find it particularly testing to not investigate any area that may hold something of interest.**

The training methods for teaching a dog to get over a fence or wall are slightly different to teaching a dog to get through cover to make a retrieve on open ground, but there are some common aspects. The first is that you need to build up the dog's confidence and that means start off with simple exercises and don't stretch the dog too far too quickly. The second is to make sure the dog always succeeds. In the early stages of training any new exercise it is really important that the dog always manages to successfully complete the task. Finally, it is always better to build up the complexity of the exercise

An inexperienced dog can get 'held up' by what it sees as a barrier and this can be an open hedge line, grass ride in a wood or stand of trees.

in gradual steps over a period of time and if the dog does struggle always be prepared to take a step back and make it easier for the dog.

The easiest way to start training a dog to go through a hedge or a rough area of cover into open ground is by utilising a basic memory retrieve. Walk the dog to heel, go through the cover or a gap in a hedge, throw out the dummy and walk back through the obstacle. Initially do not go too far from the edge of the hedge or cover, line the dog up and send it immediately. By

Training a dog to get over an obstacle is slightly different from teaching a dog to go through an obstacle, but there are some common training aspects.

getting the dog out quickly you are keeping it keen, and this will help to drive it through the cover. Gradually increase the distance that you are sending the dog from the cover but at this stage keep the retrieve fairly close to the far side of the cover or hedge. If possible, use the same location. Dogs learn by repetition and success and at the same time you are helping to build the dog's confidence. Once you are happy the dog has grasped the concept of the exercise, you can then increase the distance that you throw out the dummy from the back of the obstacle. Remember to start with sending the dog from quite close to the cover and gradually build up the distance again.

The next step is to put out a blind retrieve, one the dog hasn't seen, and repeat the exercise. You should find that because of the repetition of the previous exercise the dog will manage this part of the training without too much effort, but if it struggles you may need to go back and just recap on the memory retrieves. Over time build up the dog's experience by repeating the training exercise in different places with varying types of obstacles. The key to success is not to let the dog hunt the cover or the bottom of the hedge. If it does start to cast about call it back and set up the task again. Be consistent with this aspect of the exercise.

There is one aspect of the countryside that is the bane of every gundog owner's life and that is barbed wire. It is even worse if you have one of the

By using a simple memory retrieve exercise, you can begin to train your gundog to run through any perceived barriers.

Once the dog has the confidence to run a line you can then increase the thickness of the cover or distance that you send the dog.

smaller breeds of gundog such as a cocker spaniel. These little dogs have such heart they will try and scale any obstacle. There is a train of thought that if you never teach or encourage your dog to jump that is no bad thing especially if you do have a lot of barbed wire in your area. Little dogs can be easily lifted over if need be but if your dog is out on a retrieve and has learnt to look for a gap either in the obstacle or underneath it that is a real advantage. This aspect of the dog's training is what can be considered more advanced and in truth can be left until later in the training programme. The dog will need to be a confident retriever and be steady to a thrown dummy or cold game. He should also have a solid sit/stay as he will need to be totally steady when you climb over the fence or obstacle. Like all training exercises you need to make it simple and easier to start with and then you can gradually build up the difficulty once the dog has more confidence in what you are asking it to do.

On the face of it teaching a dog to get 'under' a wire fence or even a wooden gate sounds fairly straightforward, but it is surprising how many dogs just get totally confused and end up standing on their hind legs with their front feet on the obstacle looking quite dumb. If you have a lot of stock (sheep) fencing in your area, as many shoots will have, you can start by teaching your dog how to get under the bottom wire.

Find an area of fence that has a bit of give in the bottom of it or even better has an existing wild-animal run going underneath. First of all, sit the dog one side and then you climb over, so you are on the opposite side to the dog. Indicate with a low hand action the area which you want the dog to come underneath, use the command 'get under'. If the dog is struggling to understand what is required, you may find that if you push your hand underneath the fence this will quite often help the dog to get its head down. Once the dog has got its head down you will need to give it plenty of encouragement for it to push itself under the fence. Repeat the exercise a few times and you should find that the dog will quickly learn what you are asking it to do. When the dog is confident you can come to the same side and repeat the exercise. You may find that the dog is a bit hesitant to start with but keep up the praise and hopefully it will quickly learn through repetition; no matter what side of the obstacle you are on the dog needs to do the same action.

Another useful skill is to teach your dog to go through an obstacle and this is particularly useful if there are gaps in an old fence line or even through a closed gate that they can't get underneath. The process is the same as before: sit the dog on the opposite side of the fence, indicate the gap with your hand and call the dog through. In most cases you will be asking the dog

Teaching a dog to get under a wire fence can be especially useful if you have one of the smaller breeds.

to get through or under a fence line to go for a retrieve, so it makes sense to practise this as well. Once the dog has got the idea of either going under or through a gap, set up a simple retrieve. Initially set this up as a memory retrieve, so take the dog to the fence encourage it through the gap to the other side and throw out the dummy. Take the dog back through the gap, set it up and send the dog. There is a simple reason not to throw the dummy over the fence, and this is because it may encourage the dog to try and jump over as it will want to follow the flight of the dummy rather than go through the obstacle. Just be aware that some dogs will find it difficult coming back with a retrieve in their mouth, so they may need a bit of encouragement until they are confident in the task.

Sheep netting and barbed wire topped fences are everywhere in the countryside and as a general rule do not ask your dog to jump a barbed wire fence. Too many dogs get injured due to being caught up on wire. To be fair, a Labrador should be able to clear a fence without touching the top strand, but many dogs prefer to climb the wire, and this is where they can get caught up. Jumping puts a lot of strain on a dog's joints and limbs and therefore the dog should be physically able to deal with the strain of this exercise. First of all, you should ask yourself whether you even need to teach your dog to jump.

If you decide that you do need to teach your dog to jump, then a good way to begin is to use a fence topped with a solid wooden rail. First, sit the

It is sometimes safer for a gundog to go through an obstacle rather than trying to go over it especially in an area where there is a lot of barbed wire.

To encourage a dog to jump a wooden rail fence, straddle either side of the rail and encourage the dog to 'get over'.

Inexperienced dogs can find it more difficult jumping with something in their mouths, so to begin with use a light dummy or ball.

When the dog has gained in confidence you can throw a dummy over the fence and send the dog for the retrieve.

dog on one side of the fence and straddle the fence. Encourage it over to the other side using the command 'get over'. If the dog is a bit reluctant you can try throwing a dummy for it and this can be enough to give the dog the encouragement to jump over. Once the dog has picked the retrieve step back over the fence and use the recall whistle to call the dog back to you. Most dogs find it a bit more difficult to jump with something in their mouths so it can be a good idea to use something nice and light for the dog. If you do not have access to this kind of jump, then you could make one out of the plastic netting that is used on builders' sites. This can be set up quite easily using electric fence stakes and the height can be adjusted depending on the dog's ability and size.

As with all these exercises, gradually build up the height but don't overface the dog as if it trips or falls it can really knock the dog's confidence and it can even put them off jumping. If you are planning to use obstacles outside your training ground always check the landing side to make sure it is safe, especially if you are not familiar with the area. It is also best to try and train on level ground as it is always more difficult for a dog to jump from higher to lower ground and vice versa. This is the kind of situation where injuries can easily occur. One final thing: when working in the shooting field, if possible, consider taking the retrieve from the dog before it tries jumping back over to you especially if your gundog is one of the smaller breeds.

# 14. Scent and Lines

A cold frosty day can result in there being very little scent and as a result conditions can be quite testing for a gundog.

Understanding scent and scenting conditions can really make a difference when working gundogs. In truth that should read trying to understand scent and scenting conditions can make a difference, because as humans it is impossible to fully appreciate the power of a dog's nose. The question of scent is a subject that can confuse even the most experienced handlers. Imagine it is the last drive of the day and a couple of partridge have been shot and fallen on some plough. The air temperature is dropping very fast, and a cold mist is beginning to fall, you think the scenting conditions are quite good, but you watch as two dogs fail to pick their retrieves; both of them run straight over the top of the birds. You may be quite frustrated by the failure of your dog to make what appears to you to be a straightforward retrieve, however the dropping temperature combined with the mist has reduced the scenting conditions to nil and the dogs couldn't see the birds because the partridge blended into the plough. Being able to understand and read the conditions will consequently make you a better gundog handler.

It is generally accepted that on hot, dry days the scenting conditions for any dog will be poor, also if it is pouring with rain it can make conditions very difficult. As a handler you should take the conditions into consideration and make allowances for your dog if they are having trouble picking up the scent of shot bird. The other factor that is all too often overlooked is the wind and its direction. A good piece of advice for anyone who is planning to work a gundog is to go and watch an experienced HPR handler. Handlers of hunt, point, retrieve breeds are always checking and assessing the wind direction to help ensure they get the best out of their dogs' hunting abilities. You may even see some handlers use little talc puffers to check the wind direction or throw a handful of grass up into the air and you would be surprised how the wind, and any scent can eddy around trees and bushes at ground level. Is this important? Well yes, it is. Imagine you have a bird dropped by a tree in a field and the wind is coming from left to right. Logic dictates you should send your dog downwind of the bird, but the breeze may be disturbed by the tree and therefore any scent from the bird may not necessarily be distributed downwind, and consequently the dog may have trouble finding the bird.

**Handlers of hunt, point, retrieve breeds are always checking and assessing the wind direction ...**

On the subject of scent an experienced dog will be able to distinguish between fresh or hot-foot scent from uninjured birds and the scent from a shot bird that is either dead or injured. When you think about it a dead bird will be giving off a blood scent but also there will be the gunpowder residue from the pellets, whereas an injured bird will also be emitting endorphins, a natural pain killer, and adrenaline. You may notice that when a dog is on the line of a runner it seems to increase its pace quite significantly and this could be because the natural instincts of the dog kicks in and it reverts to a

An experienced dog will be able to tell the difference between a pricked bird and one that is uninjured. It is remarkable that these runners are retrieved back to hand.

predator tracking injured prey, fortunately for most of us when the dog finds a runner it doesn't kill and eat it, but it retrieves it back to the handler and this alone is quite remarkable.

A grouse moor in high summer has to be one of the most hostile environments for any gundog and the scenting conditions can be absolutely awful. The dogs will have to contend with the dry heat coupled with clouds of heather pollen. Add to this that when the grouse are shot, they can be quite literally buried in the heather, and it is incredible that the dogs can locate any bird by its scent. As scent is carried on moisture droplets any extreme conditions such as very hot weather, severe frost or high winds will make the scenting conditions poor, but a good gundog handler will always trust his dog to work things out, and that makes the difference. As humans we will never fully understand scent and scenting conditions but by watching as many dogs work as possible, we can at least gain a bit of knowledge and experience to help us in our training.

One element of a gundog's training that is often overlooked is the teaching of taking a line and in truth it is one of the most important skills that any gundog used to retrieve game should be taught. However, this can be rather confusing for the dog especially if it is one of the breeds that are predominantly bred to hunt rather than retrieve. The main contradiction

is that during the dog's early hunting and quartering training you will be discouraging it from pulling forward on scent lines as this will disrupt the dog's hunting pattern and then when you start to teach the dog to take a scent line, you are encouraging the dog to do exactly what you have been training it not to do: a true contradiction.

So, the question has to be asked, 'Why bother potentially confusing the dog in this way?' In reality the answer is quite simple. It is a fact that no matter how good you are at shooting or if you are picking up on a driven shoot you will inevitably come across a situation where game has not been killed outright and has run on. It is your and your dog's responsibility to do your best to find it and to humanely dispatch it as quickly as possible. That is why we have well-trained gundogs. You should be able to get your dog to the area in which the bird has landed or in the case of ground game, it was shot. The dog should then work out the direction its quarry ran and follow that line. When they get it right it is one of the most exciting things to watch. Some dogs have a natural ability to do this, but most need be taught. Before you can begin these lessons, your dog must be a reliable retriever. You will

A grouse moor in the height of summer can be a hostile environment for gundog work. Pollen, heat and very little scent can make for extremely testing conditions.

Shot scent is something a gundog has to learn to recognise and creating scent lines for the dog can give them experience on injured game.

have already built the foundations of these exercises by using tennis and fur balls and then moving on to cold game and by gradually make the exercises more challenging for the dogs. Not everyone has access to ground where they can shoot over their dogs, especially when training them; however, you can still get your dog used to taking lines of shot game albeit cold game and artificial shot scent. Most handlers will have either a dummy launcher or a starting pistol so you can fire a blank onto a dead bird or rabbit. Then you can drag the retrieve on the end of a rope to create a scent line. Obviously do this whilst the dog is out of sight.

It is interesting to watch how dogs use their noses and, of course, different gundog breeds work in slightly different ways. It is quite noticeable that on warm days when the grass has a heavy covering of dew, dogs that normally work with their noses to the ground such as retrievers and spaniels will lift their heads slightly. This is because as the sun starts to warm up the wet grass, the water molecules begin to evaporate along with the scent of the retrieve; consequently the dog may be picking up the line above the ground. The HPR breeds, along with setters and pointers and even flat-coated and golden retrievers, all work with a higher head carriage and generally work on air scent rather than ground scent but, of course, they can adapt their styles to the conditions.

As with all new exercises you will begin by making things simple so the dog doesn't fail, as this helps to build up confidence. Sit the dog next to you and using a heavyweight fur ball roll it out in front of the dog so at this stage it will be a simple 'seen' retrieve. Use an area of rough grass and if possible, on a slight hill as this will help the ball to roll further. Ideally do this exercise on a day that the ground is either wet or at least damp. Try to avoid warm dry conditions as there will be less scent left by the rolling ball. Send the dog and observe its body language. You should see it lower its head as it hits the area where the ball landed and rolled. Start off with a short throw and gradually increase the distance you roll the ball. Once your dog is confidently going out and following the 'seen' lines it is time to make things a little bit more challenging. Sit the dog next to you and once again roll the ball out in front of you, but just before it lands cover the dog's eyes with one hand. The dog will know something has been thrown for it, but it won't have had the chance to see it land. Send your dog and it should run out to the area it last saw the ball, the 'fall area'. As soon as the dog begins to hunt the area give it plenty of encouragement.

As with many exercises start simply. Rolling a heavy tennis ball down a hill will help to teach a dog to follow a line.

Although you can teach the dog the skills needed using artificial means you should be very cautious when the time comes to set the dog off on the real thing. You will spend a lot of time and effort in training your gundog and during their first season you should be careful to make sure you don't overface the dog and put it in a situation where its training could quickly become unravelled. Picking your dog's first runner is a classic point in case.

Imagine you are picking up with your dog, you are watching him to make sure he is steady to falling birds and unshot birds that are landing nearby and then you see a pricked bird that lands and runs. Now you have a decision to make. If you have an older more experienced dog with you it

Make sure you drag the retrieve at arm's length to help prevent any foot scent on the line.

would be advisable to send that and let the youngster watch. If not, you could take a chance and send the young dog. The main issue that could arise here is that if the bird is a strong late season cock bird it may prove too challenging for an inexperienced dog. If the dog does get hold of it and the bird kicks out with its spurs this could encourage the dog to squeeze a little bit harder to stop the bird and then you potentially have a dog that may become hard mouthed. The bottom line is to choose your retrieves wisely; don't be rushed into anything and let your dog gradually gain experience and confidence. Watching a dog take the line of a runner is one of the most exciting aspects of gundog work but it does need to be practised on the training field.

In the previous exercise you have been concentrating on rolling balls to create a reasonably short scent line for the dog to follow. Now it is time to increase the complexity of the line. When game is shot there will be a number of scents given off: blood, adrenaline and shot residue from the pellets. You can teach the dog to recognise shot scent by firing a starting pistol onto a rabbit-skin dummy or some cold game. Do this at the beginning of the drag to create a fall area. Once you have created the fall area you can then proceed to lay the line. Initially, drag the dummy or game alongside a hedge, as it will help the dog by giving it a straight line to follow. Tie the lure to a long line and drag it in a straight line at arm's length as this helps avoid getting any foot scent on the line. Initially don't make it too far. When you reach the end rub the 'retrieve' in the ground again to make another hotspot. Leave a dummy or cold game for the dog to retrieve.

When you line up your dog make sure you are working into the wind. This will make it easier for the dog and help to increase its confidence. You are looking for the dog to get its nose down on the scent line, so indicate with your hand the first fall area and with luck the dog should follow the line like a train on a track. Once your dog is confidently following artificial lines you can progress to cold game which will, of course, add another element of scent into the exercise. Set the task up exactly as you did previously with the dummy but this time you can add in some bends or even take it through a gap in the hedge line.

Another training scenario is to set out your drag line as in the previous exercises, but this time try sending your dog across the line of scent rather than setting it off at the beginning of the line. Obviously, your dog will have to work out which way the line runs, and it may take a few casts before the dog does this, but it will all add to the dog's experience. In the shooting field you may not always be able to put your dog right on the area of the fall, so it is good practice to be prepared for any situation that you may come across in the future.

To really test your dog, you can make these exercises as complex as you like, and it helps if you can think like a pricked bird. When picking up, the Guns may be standing out in a grass field so any injured birds will make for

Use a low hand signal to get the dog's nose down on the simulated 'fall' area.

whatever cover there is available so try and set up these scenarios. If there is a tree or a rough area in the field, lay a line from the grass back into the cover: it is exactly where a pricked bird would run. Send the dog from the fall area in the field and let it work out which direction the bird has taken. The more experience you can give the dog in a training scenario the better equipped it will be when you take it out into the shooting field.

As the dog grows in confidence you can make the drag lines more complex. Try and think like a pricked bird that has been shot and is looking for cover.

# 15. Working With Another Dog

When working multiple dogs, it is important that each one knows its job and has been trained to respect the others in the team.

Anyone that works or trains gundogs will tell you they are very addictive and once you have one you will want another, then another and then probably ... well, another! This will especially be the case if you want to go picking up. In fact, many shoots will insist that if you aspire to join their picking-up team, having more than one dog will be a necessary requirement. As with any form of gundog training there are going to be varying degrees of what a handler deems acceptable in how their dogs work. For some handlers they are content with keeping their team on leads during a drive and then letting them all go when the horn is sounded. It is far more efficient to have your picking-up dogs off the lead, once they are trained obviously. That way you can send individual dogs for any pricked birds at any time without the hassle of trying to get a slip lead off. It should be said that working two or more untrained dogs together is asking for trouble and not only can it end up being very chaotic but also highly embarrassing. We have all seen two dogs chasing each other during sweeping up, one with a bird in its mouth and the other one desperately trying to snatch it back out. Even worse is witnessing a tug of war between picking-up dogs: not only does it look bad and renders the shot game inedible this also has the potential to escalate into an aggressive situation.

If you are going to work more than one dog it is important that they understand they are part of a team, but they will also have to work individually and be respectful of the other canine members of a picking-up team. There is one very good reason to practise and train your dogs to work in this kind of scenario. During a drive birds will be shot dead, and some will be pricked and end up being runners. If you can send individual dogs out to individual retrieves whilst keeping other dogs back in reserve, it makes the collection of shot game far more effective. When a particular dog comes back with a bird the other dogs should ignore it and concentrate on waiting for their next command. If the other waiting dogs start to bother the incoming dog, they may well miss the mark of another shot bird. More importantly, you as the handler will not be able to concentrate on the dog making the retrieve.

... even worse is witnessing a tug of war between picking-up dogs ...

Teaching a dog to work with another one or indeed in a team of dogs is a skill that certainly needs practice, and you almost have to desensitise the new dog to the situation. Although there are no hard and fast rules as to when to introduce this exercise, the dog needs to be steady to thrown dummies, have a solid 'sit/stay' command and also be used to having a lead on. It is also strongly recommended you do these exercises with an older experienced dog which can be sent for the initial retrieves. If you do not have a reliable older dog seek the help of a friend or a professional trainer that does have one. It is also really important that your frame of mind is right as

Initially when training this exercise keep the trainee dog on the lead and use a more experienced dog to make the retrieve.

you will need to stay very calm and not get wound up as this exercise can get quite fractious.

You must set up this training exercise to ensure you limit the chance of failure with the younger dog. Initially put the trainee on a lead and sit the dog right next to you, throw out a dummy and send the older dog. Keep your eye on the restrained dog and as the retriever comes back just give a quick tug on the lead and the command 'leave it'. If need be, use your body to block the sitting dog from being able to snatch or lunge at the incoming dog.

Once your young dog is proving steady on the lead you can progress to the next stage. Sit the dog slightly behind you and slightly to one side. Throw out your retrieve and at the same time reinforce steadiness by putting out your hand and again use the 'leave it' command. When working more than one dog it is better to use the dog's name to send it for a retrieve as this helps to prevent any misunderstanding on the dog's behalf. As you send the experienced dog watch the youngster as the trigger point will be as the other dog launches off. Because you have positioned the dog slightly behind, you are already in a position to block the dog should it decide to run in. If it does move, try to stop it, and put it back on the spot it moved from and reinforce the 'sit' command.

At some point you will have to up the temptation by using some cold game. This will also most certainly increase the possibility that the young dog will try and snatch it from the older dog. To begin with get the experienced dog to hold on to a partridge or pheasant and sit it up in front of you with the young dog just off to one side. Be in no hurry to take the bird, and constantly watch the young dog to gauge its reaction.

Once things have progressed and you are happy that the young dog has learnt the exercise you can reverse things and send it for a retrieve whilst the older dog sits next to you. The one thing you have to watch out for is that the inexperienced dog may well want to parade around showing off to the older dog, so block the young retriever from getting to the older dog thus preventing the situation happening in the first place.

Sit the younger dog slightly behind and be ready to use your body to block the dog should it run in.

A further progression of this exercise is to eventually send both dogs for individual retrieves at the same time. Obviously the younger dog has to have fully learnt the earlier lessons before moving on to this stage of its training. Initially throw out two dummies in the opposite direction, one in front and one behind you. Make one of the retrieves shorter than the other. Send the younger dog first for the closer dummy and when it is on the way out send the older dog for the further retrieve. The idea behind this is that the younger dog will be back with its dummy before the older one so you can get it sitting and settled before the experienced dog comes back to you. As you further develop this exercise you can throw the retrieves closer together to the point where you can put a number of retrieves out in an area and send both dogs at the same time and they should work independently of each other.

Over time the young dog will learn to ignore the retrieving dog and not make any effort to snatch the dummy.

When introducing the temptation of cold game, concentrate on the younger dog whilst the experienced dog sits in front holding the retrieve.

# 16. Directions

To prevent your gundog pre-empting your hand signals you should spend time desensitising the dog ... never let the dog second-guess you.

Being able to direct your gundog in the shooting field is not only a useful skill but should be considered a necessary skill, unless perhaps you only plan to go beating with your dog. Many novices think that being able to send your dog left, right or back is something that you only need to teach one of the retrieving breeds but although you may not need to send a spaniel quite as far away as a Labrador there will certainly be occasions when you need to be able to direct any breed of gundog to a certain point, especially if you plan to go picking up or if you are going to shoot over your dog. There are basically three directions you need to teach your dog: left, right and back. Just be aware that when training these particular exercises, the dog can quickly begin to anticipate what you are going to do as soon as you lift or move your arms. It is good practice to desensitise the dog by waving your arms about, set things up as though you are going to send it and then pull your arms back down and sometimes walk back to the dog or call it into you. Remember that golden rule ... never let the dog second-guess what you are going to ask it to do.

The go back exercise can put a lot of physical pressure on a dog as you will be asking it to almost swivel 180 degrees to go out for a retrieve and therefore you really do not want to start teaching this until the dog is mature enough so that its bones, ligaments, and muscles are well developed. You will not be able to begin teaching this exercise until your dog is completely steady to thrown dummies and can sit and stay at a distance from you for a reasonable length of time. You must make sure that these basics are in place – if not there is the possibility the dog will break and self-reward itself by getting to the dummy long before you can get to the dog and once the dog has the dummy you will not be able to correct it. Remember, prevention is better than cure.

The 'go back' command basically means that the dog should turn around 180 degrees and go out in a line away from the handler. Ideally the dog should keep going until it either finds or winds the retrieve or is stopped and given another command. Obviously, you cannot expect the dog to run arrow-straight, but it should be there or thereabouts, and you do not want it running off at an angle. You will need to be consistent when teaching this exercise. If the dog runs off at an angle you must stop it, put it back on the original spot and set the task up again. Don't fall into the common habit of stopping the dog, trying to send it right or left and then trying the back again. The exercise is for the dog to go straight back, and this is the lesson you need to teach it, not allowing it to do a zigzag pattern.

The first consideration when teaching the go back is the training location. You should always make matters as easy as possible for the dog

... never let the dog second-guess what you are going to ask it to do.

The use of a track will help to guide your dog when training the 'go-back' command.

as your aim should be to increase their confidence by allowing them to succeed. Failure teaches them nothing. Preferably, you should use a track that will help to guide the dog in the early stages of learning the exercise. It is a good idea to try and include as many elements as possible to the dog's training in one exercise and when setting up your 'go back' command you can walk the dog out whilst at heel, throw out a dummy whilst telling the dog to 'leave it' and then walk away again at heel. Initially sit the dog around 15 metres from the dummy and then walk on a further 5 or 10 metres. In just this one exercise you have already combined heelwork, steadiness work, a sit/stay and you have set up a memory retrieve.

Ultimately any hand signal you give the dog will be at a distance and if you are working one of the retrieving breeds it could be at a significant distance, so you must get into good habits from the beginning. A mistake that is often made is that the handler fails to give clear signals to the dog, and this can be the case where the hand signal is concerned. Make sure you are making a good separation between your arms and hands and your body. If you put your hand in front of your face it will be nigh on impossible for the dog to see the command at any kind of distance, so make sure you give a clear signal with your hand up high and slightly to one side.

You must make sure that the dog is looking at you before giving the command and hand signal. A good way to achieve this is to give a little peep on your whistle. This will draw the dog's attention to you ... you could think of it as almost a look at me command. When you are ready push up your hand with the verbal cue of 'go back'. The first couple of times you may find the dog is a bit sticky and won't go. This is not unusual as it is a new lesson. Try taking a step forward at the same time and generally this movement will be enough to make the dog turn and head out towards the dummy. Over time you can gradually increase the distance between you and the dog.

Once your dog has fully grasped the exercise you can then move on to more testing ground, but you still have to give some thought to making the transition as easy as possible. If possible, try and find a field with a fence line that runs into a corner. This will give the dog a guide and a boundary to follow. Repeat the exercise as you did on the track. By putting the dummy in the corner of the fence it gives the dog a confined target area to work in and this will help to increase its confidence. You can then gradually move the dog away from the fence line into the open field but at the same time keeping the dummy in the same place. You should find that by repetition of the verbal and visible command the dog will soon learn that when it hears and sees the instructions, it needs to turn about and it will find a retrieve.

One fundamental aspect of working a gundog is that you should have the ability to retrieve game whether it is dead or injured and in the latter case your dog should be competent enough to make that retrieve quickly and efficiently. In theory, if you can send your dog back in a straight line you shouldn't have to train it to go right and left as providing you can line it up directly to the retrieve the dog should keep running until you either stop it or it finds the retrieve. An essential element to successful gundog training is eye contact. If you cannot get your dog to look at you then you will find it very difficult to progress to any great degree and you will have no chance of introducing any form of directional handling. You want to develop a relationship where the dog works with its natural ability but also trusts you as the handler and this can be developed from an early age.

Make sure all your hand signals are clear and precise as you will eventually be directing your dog at a distance.

Once the dog is ready for proper directional training the method is straightforward. First of all, sit the dog up against a hedge or fence line. At this stage only walk back a short distance and throw a dummy to either the right or left side of the dog. It is important that the dummy lands level with the dog's position. As with all gundog commands, directional hand signals

When moving to a more open training area you can initially use a fence line to help guide the dog and help increase its confidence.

should be clear and precise. If you think about it, out in the shooting field you could be handling your dog at a considerable distance and therefore you need to make sure the dog can see you. When you are ready to send your dog take a step in the direction and put out your arm, keep your hand flat to the dog as this will visually help the dog. It important that you do not pull your arm back too quickly.

As mentioned before, when sending a dog for a retrieve it is good practice to use a release command. As you push out your hand give your verbal retrieving command and this helps to encourage the dog to run out to the dummy. One problem that can occur when sending a dog left or right is that it can drift back towards the handler at an angle rather than running out at right angles to the handler. This is quite often due to poor training technique, or the dog is lacking in confidence. To begin with stay quite close to the dog as this will help to prevent the dog from coming back towards you at an angle. As the dog gains in confidence, you can gradually increase the distance between you and the dog but for the time being keep the thrown dummy quite close. To begin with just concentrate on either the left or right direction and make sure the dog really understands the task before changing sides.

Once the dog is solid on both individual left and rights and you have managed to move a fair distance away from it, you can then begin to put out retrieves either side of the dog. The rule here is to always send the dog for the first one you threw out, as the dog will naturally want to go for the last one. A little trick to help the dog is to throw the first one a bit closer to the dog and the last one a bit further away. When you are standing in front of the dog it can also help if you just take a step to the side you are going to send the dog, and this will encourage the dog to go that way. Just be ready in case the dog picks the first dummy and runs towards the second one. You can help prevent this from happening by simply moving to the spot where the dog

When introducing left and right commands it can be beneficial to position the dog in front of a fence line or hedge to help guide them and teach them to run at right angles.

was set up as it is out on the retrieve and that way you are blocking the dog from running towards the second dummy. Mix this exercise up, change directions, go and pick some of the retrieves yourself, sometimes even call the dog back into you. Remember, keep them guessing. The ultimate aim is to be able to throw out left, right, and back retrieves and send the dog for whichever one you choose.

A dog can also quite easily become overhandled. This is a situation where the dog relies more on the handler and his directional commands than on its natural instincts. Unfortunately this is a trait that is being seen more and more in competition dogs. The dog should never be able to pre-empt your commands and unless you are thorough in your training methods it can be all too easy for the dog to move as soon as you lift your arms. This is a form of unsteadiness and is easily avoided by adding a verbal release command.

You can emphasise the direction you want to send the dog by taking a step to one side at the same time as pushing your arm out in the required direction.

# 17. Water Work

Swimming or the use of a hydro-treadmill is a great way of getting your gundog fit for the rigours of the shooting season.

As with all aspects of a gundog's training water work needs to be done carefully and with thought. It is all too easy to end up with numerous problems such as dropping retrieves, shaking and even the refusal to enter water. Of course, it is a matter of choice whether you train your dog to retrieve from water. If you are in an area that has little or no water and it is unlikely that your dog would ever need that skill, then you may consider it unnecessary.

However, getting your dog to enjoy swimming has other benefits. Swimming is a great way of getting a dog really fit and ready for the rigours of the shooting field. Also, because water resistance is greater than air resistance, the muscles have to work harder. It is said that for a dog, one minute's swimming is equivalent to about four minutes of running. Some handlers are now using hydrotherapy as a supplementary form of exercise to improve strength, stamina, and firmness. Once used to swimming, most dogs just simply enjoy it. Stronger, toned muscles will help to protect your dog against injuries that can be sustained during hunting, jumping, and working in testing conditions.

If you plan to pick up with your dog or even shoot over it then the chances are you will need the dog to be able to retrieve from water, but always be cautious. Always consider the conditions before sending your dog in any water especially in the winter months. A cocker with a thin coat will not cope very well with entering freezing water and then being asked to sit through a drive soaking wet. Never send your dog for a retrieve if a river is running fast or in flood and no matter how strong a swimmer your dog may be, and never ask it to go into a lake or pond with ice on top. You are just asking for trouble. Although it looks spectacular, a dog that leaps into the water can cause itself a nasty injury from underwater obstacles, so always check to make sure there are no branches or old shopping trollies laying just underneath the water before sending your dog in. It's not unusual where a Gun points out that there is a retrieve in the water, and everyone decides to send their dogs in for it and it becomes a competition. The best course of action in a case like this is to call your dog to heel and pop it on a lead if need be and not get involved in a free-for-all. It will do your dog no good at all.

> **Never send your dog for a retrieve if a river is running fast or in flood …**

The question as to when you should start doing some water training is simply answered with – when the weather warms up and the pup is a confident retriever. Of course, you could encourage the little dog have a paddle about from quite a young age and most dogs take to the water like ducks. However, if your dog is a bit cautious under no circumstances force the dog into the water as you may well put it off for life. Patience, persistence, and persuasion are the keys to success. Firstly find a suitable water location. It should ideally

Although a gundog leaping into water can look spectacular you should always ensure there are no underwater obstacles that may cause an injury.

be a still or very slow-moving area of water and it should be a warm day. It is not a good idea to try and get your dog keen on water if it is going to get freezing cold and wet. Also avoid steep banks with muddy or silty bottoms. These exercises are all about building up the dog's confidence and avoiding any situations that may scare them.

Some young dogs simply lack the confidence to go from firm ground into water and this is probably because they cannot see the bottom, which is why it is important that you find a shallow location with a firm bottom. Many handlers will initially try and send the dog from the bank, but it is better to put on a pair of wellies and walk out a few steps into the water and encourage the pup towards you. To start with make sure you are close to the water and that there is a gently sloping bank to the water's edge. Give the dog a retrieve or two on the water's edge; this allows the youngster to pick the dummy with four paws on firm ground. If this is successful put the dummy out a little further. It is better to use one of the rubber waterproof ones. Avoid using canvas dummies as they get waterlogged and quite heavy, although dummies made of Cordura tend to be a bit better. And remember, always check the bank and water for any obstructions. You can keep your dog

If your gundog is reluctant to enter water, don a pair of wellies and go for a paddle. Make sure you use a shallow location with a firm bottom.

on a lead to enable a more controlled entry. Ideally, set this up with the wind blowing the scent of the dummy into the dog's face to give it a little more encouragement. If you feel the dog lacks confidence after a certain depth or is reluctant to go the final step and swim, do not keep pushing it; leave it for that session and start again another day. If your young dog is reluctant to enter the water, you could employ the help of a more experienced dog. First of all, call out the older dog and give the dog a bit of fuss this can create a little bit of jealously and nine times out of ten the younger dog will find that

Give the dog a few straightforward retrieves using a suitable dummy. If you stand in the water the dog is less likely to drop and shake.

irresistible and come in to join you. You can then walk off up the stream and call both dogs with you and more often than not the young dog will trot along quite happily.

By far the most common fault with water work is the dog dropping the retrieve when making the delivery. The best way to get a good habit into the dog is to initially stand in the water and call the dog back into you. Most dogs are unlikely to shake when still in the water. Once your dog is doing this reliably you can move on to the next stage. You will need to find an area where the dog can get an easy exit to the bank, throw out your retrieve and send the dog. You need to be positioned close to the bank edge but far enough back so the dog can get onto firm ground. Once the dog is confidently coming back to you, gradually move back further away from the bank and each time make sure you give the dog lots of encouragement. If your dog starts to drop short move a few steps forward and work on that distance until you get a reliable delivery.

When your dog is swimming confidently it is a good idea to think about making the retrieves more challenging. In the shooting field there may be occasions when you will need to send your dog over water, either to the far bank or perhaps to an island. Injured ducks will try and hide in any cover alongside the bank, so you want your dog to learn to not always look for

Initially, position yourself right on the water's edge so the dog gets used to coming out of the water without dropping the retrieve. You can then gradually move further back.

retrieves on the open water. Start with simple seen retrieves thrown over the water to the far bank. You will, of course, have to find a suitable location where the water isn't too wide and not running too fast. Just as you built up the dog's memory and the blind retrieves in the previous exercises you can do the same in this instance. Use the same location to increase the dog's confidence before moving on to a different area.

Don't fall into the trap of always putting your water retrieves in open water. You will need to practise sending your dog over water either to the far bank or even an island.

# 18. Picking Up

**Picking up on a shoot comes with responsibility and quite often a handler and their dogs will be the last to leave the shooting field.**

It can be 'heart in the mouth' stuff sending a dog for a runner during a drive. It will depend on the particular shoot whether this is acceptable or not ... always check first.

How to join a picking-up team on a shoot is a question that is often asked and to be honest there is no definitive answer, but once you have managed to secure a place you will have certain responsibilities to the shoot and more importantly to any game that is shot. Most shoots and especially the bigger ones may want you to have more than one dog, as the main function will be to sweep up after a drive and the job needs to be done as quickly and as efficiently as possible. The question does get asked, what breed of gundog is best for picking up? Well, the obvious answer would be a retriever such as a Labrador, golden or flat-coated retriever but both the HPR breeds and spaniels certainly have their place, and in an ideal world your team would be a mixture but there are more important things than the breed of dog you have.

Before starting your day check with the head picker-up as to the rules regarding sending a dog during a drive and, in particular, the situation regarding runners. Each shoot and indeed each drive may be different and that is why it is always worth checking. It may be that on one drive the Guns are over the other side of a small lane in another field, so it is fine to pick runners during the drive before they reach the sanctuary of any cover, but ordinarily you wouldn't pick dead birds until the drive has finished. You never know who is watching and therefore always be aware of that fact and act accordingly. That includes 'reprimanding' your dog and the dispatching of game properly. On most shoots the pickers-up must carry 'priests' and they have to be used. The use of fence posts and tree trunks should not be tolerated, and neither should swinging a bird by its neck. Shooting is under enough pressure as it is, and we owe it to our quarry that it is dispatched quickly and humanely. When arriving at the drive you will normally be shown to where you need to stand and just be aware that handlers will have their regular places and can be quite possessive over their patch of ground. Once you have been given your allocated spot make your way there with the minimum of fuss and noise. Always keep your dogs on a lead until you get to your place and then sit them up and take off their leads.

**...ordinarily you wouldn't pick dead birds until the drive has finished.**

Now there are a couple of points to bear in mind with regarding whether you keep your dog on or off a lead during a drive. Even the best-trained dog will occasionally have a blip and during a busy drive birds will be dropping all around and your dogs have to be rock-steady. You may be standing way back in a wood, in a position just at the end of the pheasant's flight path and you could get numerous birds landing through the trees. Quite often the birds will be running right under the dogs' noses and that is quite a temptation. You will need all your concentration to not only be watching your dogs but also to be on the lookout for any pricked birds because at the end of the day

Any breed of gundog can work as part as a picking-up team, but they should be well trained and be used to working together.

that is the main function of picking up, to find and humanely dispatch any injured game. If you have any doubt about your dog's steadiness, then it is better to keep them on a lead until the end of the drive. Picking up is not a competition and it is certainly not the time to show off with your dogs. Remember, a gundog's main aim in life is to make its handler look like a fool!

The positioning of your dogs during a drive also needs some consideration. If you are shooting on a driven day, the best place for your dog is about 2 metres in front and facing you. That way you can watch the dog and he can mark any shot birds that fall behind you. However, when picking up it is better to have your dog sitting either slightly in front or to one side facing the drive. That way they can see the birds coming and still get a good mark on any birds that go on behind. At some point during the day, you may have to make a very difficult decision and it is one that should not be taken lightly because it could well determine your future on the shoot. A lot will depend on whether you have been told it is okay to collect birds during

the drive and then whether you have a dog that is experienced enough to go out to a specific bird and ignore others landing around them. It really can be heart in your mouth stuff even more so if you are in sight of the Guns. Be honest with yourself and if you are not sure or if you have young dogs then do not take the chance. Just watch the bird and try and pick it after the drive has finished. You can train your dogs to deal with situations like this, but a shoot day is not the time or place: you are there to do a job. We have all had young inexperienced dogs to bring on but there are certain situations when you should leave matters to the older, better-trained members of the team although at some point you may have bite the bullet and take a calculated chance. Just choose your moment carefully.

Ideally your picking-up dogs should sit quietly off the lead so they can be sent for any pricked birds without the hassle of trying to remove a lead.

Sweeping up after a drive basically means walking forward from your position towards the Guns and picking any dead birds and retrieving any runners that have not been collected during the drive. It should be pointed out that picking up is not about who can collect the most birds. Unfortunately, there are those that like to mooch around the pegs and come back laden with birds and think they have done a good day's work. A good picker-up is the handler and their dogs that will work hard to find that pricked bird a

Gun is sure he has hit, and whether they find it or not they are willing to give it their best. Not only a cardinal sin but also damned annoying are the dogs that constantly swap game. We have all seen it: a dog is sent out and it picks up a bird and then runs off. It comes across another one and then swaps it over and does the same thing over and over again. Eventually it gets back to the handler who in most cases is none the wiser. It is well worth training your dogs to avoid this from happening but also to stop them stealing from other dogs' retrieves, which can certainly happen as all the pickers-up get close to the pegs and the dogs start to come together. Guns with their own dogs will in most cases want to pick their own birds, especially around the pegs. If you can it is always worth checking but if you can't for any reason, it is fairly safe to assume that they will pick up but still keep an eye to make sure that they do collect everything as they may well be quickly ushered to the next drive. It is also good etiquette to offer to take any birds from the Guns and when you get to the game cart, don't just dump the birds and walk off.

Stealing a retrieve or swapping retrieves is a highly undesirable trait in a picking-up dog and you should train to prevent this from happening.

You should also check how the shoot wants you to carry your birds. Some shoots may be okay with you putting them in game bags or vests, others

would prefer that you use game carriers, so the birds can cool down. If you have finished your sweep help out in tying up the birds, check how the birds need to be tied up. Most shoots will want them paired up, cock and hen, but others may want all the hens put together. It is better to ask than get it wrong. Whilst at the game cart make sure you keep an eye on your dog as some can become a bit possessive when there is a lot of game laying around and many other dogs are milling about. If you are lucky enough to get on a good shoot, over time you will get to know the routines and become a valuable member of the picking-up team. Just remember, when someone new arrives for their first day take the time to help them out and point them in the right direction; after all, we all had to start somewhere.

Above and right. If you are new to the shoot, it is worth checking how you should carry the birds. Many shoots do not like game bags as they do not allow the birds to cool down. Game carriers are the preferred option.

A dog used in the beating line has the potential to cause a major disaster and therefore should be trained to the highest standard.

# 19. Beating

The beaters' wagon can be quite intimidating for a novice gundog.

Of all the participants in a shooting day a beater with their dog has the potential to cause a major disaster and ruin a well-planned drive. Therefore, it is vitally important that both the handler and dog are not only well trained but also well versed in how a beating line works. First of all, a dog used in the beating line should hunt in a nice tight pattern under control of its handler. It should be steady to the flush of birds and not chase any ground game including deer. The dog will need to be on the whistle and that means it should respond immediately to both the stop and turn whistle. When it comes to stopping to the flush of game there are two trains of thought. Some handlers like their dogs to stop or sit each time the dog makes contact with a bird; on the other hand, some handlers are happy if the dog ignores the flush and carries on hunting, providing they remain under control. Occasionally on a shoot day you may see people beating with dogs on a lead. This is often claimed to be a case of letting the dog see what goes on. Now this is up to the gamekeeper as to whether this is acceptable, but it should be remembered that when working in the beating line on a shoot day you are there to do a job and not to train your dog. It is likely that you will achieve very little except to end up with a very frustrated dog.

A beating line can be a confusing place for a young dog. There will be a lot of other dogs, there will be a lot of noise including other handlers blowing their whistles, there will be shouting and hollering and on many shoots the beaters will be using flags. Having something waving around can be scary enough but most beaters' flags are made from plastic feed bags and are used in a way that makes a cracking sound that can be quite loud. It is a really good idea to get your dog used to hearing and seeing flags being used well before you take them beating for the first time. If you get the chance to go on a well-run beaters' workshop this can be a really good way to introduce a young dog to the sights and sounds of a shoot day. However, do make sure it is a well-run day with a trainer who can not only teach the finer points of beating but also has experience of working a dog in the beating line.

The main job of a dog in the beating line is to find and flush game for the Guns and the volume of birds on the ground will vary from shoot to shoot, but in any event your dog must be steady when faced with both flying and running birds. During the foundation training of your dog, you should have started by getting the dog steady to thrown tennis balls and dummies. Temptation can then be increased by using a rabbit pen. Rabbit pens are a great way to steady dogs under controlled conditions and there are plenty of trainers that have pens for hire, normally under their supervision. If you are on good terms with your gamekeeper, you may be able to get some dogging in later in the year. This will give your dog some real 'hands on' experience of

It is a really good idea to get your dog used to hearing and seeing flags being used …

A beating line can be a confusing place for a young dog especially if plastic flags are used. A few training sessions getting the dog used to the crack of a flag is time well spent.

flushing large numbers of birds. Just a note of caution. When faced with a lot of birds a young dog can very quickly get fired up, known as getting hot, so you need to be very aware of this and stop the exercise before things get out of control.

The beaters' wagon is probably the one thing that you cannot prepare or train your dog to deal with and it can be a very stressful environment for a young dog. Just look at it from the dog's point of view: it is crammed in with loads of humans and other unknown dogs, some of which may well be protecting their own space. You will always get the bully that will try and prove that it is top dog. Beaters' wagons also vary from shoot to shoot. You may be lucky and be transported around in a purpose-built trailer, or on the other hand it may be the back of a pickup. No matter what the mode of transport there are some ways you can make things less stressful for a novice dog.

If the shoot uses a trailer, then sit at the end. That way the dog will be able to see out and will only have one neighbour. Most trailers have steep steps, and these can be difficult for a young dog to negotiate. If your dog is having trouble getting up, then just lift it up. Don't make a big issue of it. Also, when getting back out of the trailer get someone to hold on to the dog whilst you climb down and then lift the dog out; don't let it jump. Keep your dog on a lead at all times when in the trailer and especially if you are travelling in the back of a pickup.

One of the issues that you may come across when working a dog in the beating line is that in most cases the line will walk to the speed of beaters without dogs and that tends to be a bit too fast. This can cause the dog to push on too quickly. It can be difficult trying to watch your dog and at the same time making sure you are staying in line with your fellow beaters. You do have to have eyes in the back of your head. Ideally you want to give your dog time to work the cover especially bramble patches. If you think about it a dogless beater will give a patch of bramble a few quick whacks with their stick and move on, whereas your dog will want to get in and have a good thrash about and if there are lots of brambles it won't take long before you find you are behind the line. Consequently, if you move on too quickly your dog will soon learn to avoid hunting the cover and just run around it. If there are a lot of dogs working the line or the cover is thick you may well hear the keeper give the command, 'Let the dogs work,' which should indicate to the beaters

Try and position your novice gundog at the back of the beaters' wagon so it can see out but keep hold of the dog's lead.

without dogs to slow down. Do not be afraid to ask the line to slow down a bit if there are areas that need dogging out properly, especially on smaller shoots where every bird counts.

No matter where you go beating you will come across out of control dogs and probably more so smaller more informal shoots. The first thing to remember is that they are not your concern. However, they can affect the way your dog works. Dogs by their very nature are competitive animals and should another dog start to hunt out in front of your dog it can quickly cause yours to pull on and you want to avoid this at all costs. If you have out of control dogs hunting out in front of you, pull your own dog back into heel and keep it there until the offenders have cleared off back to their owners. Working a dog in the beating line is not a competition and you have invested a lot of time in training your dog and it is vital you maintain its discipline.

Nearly all shoots no matter what their size will have some kind of cover crops to contend with and whilst some such as wild bird mixes and root crops can be great to work the dog in, others such as canary grass and maize can be the undoing of even the best-trained dogs. First of all, you have to remember why the cover crops are in place and that in most cases they are there to hold birds that have been blanked in from a wider area; therefore, you and your dog are likely to come across a significant number of birds and you need to keep your wits about you to prevent a disaster from happening.

Over the past few years canary grass has become very popular as a holding crop. If it is topped off it can be great in which to work a dog, but quite often it is left to its own devices and becomes tall and very thick and therein lies the problem for the beater with a dog. It can be challenging to hunt your dog and see where it is whilst at the same time you need to try and keep your footing. The one advantage of canary grass is that it does hold the dogs back so they are unlikely to get too far ahead of the beating line, but they can become quickly disorientated and lose their handler. The other thing to watch out for is the dog pushing to the outside of the crop and running forward and then trying to work its way back to the beating line, the telltale sign of this happening is that birds start to flush back over the beater. Quite often someone will shout that there is a fox or deer running around the flushing point, but more often than not it is a wayward dog from the beating line. In one way maize blocks are a bit easier to deal with as the rule of thumb is quite simply keep your dog on a lead or at heel. If you hunt your dog in a stand of maize you are asking for trouble. This crop is planted in long rows, and these are like motorways for pheasants and a young novice dog is more than likely to follow the foot scent of the birds and just keep going until they get to the flushing point, and you really do not want that to happen.

Of all the situations that you will come across as a beater with a dog,

the flushing point will potentially be the area where it could all so easily go wrong. As you reach the end of the covers the chances are that there will be a large build-up of birds and even if you have been working your dog up to this point it is now that you need to have some self-discipline. First and foremost, it helps if you know the drives so you can anticipate where the flushing points are and as you work towards them call your dog back into heel or, if need be, put it on the lead. There is no shame in putting your dog on the lead. It is like taking it out of gear and putting it in neutral and more importantly you know where it is. The chances are the line will slowly work forward and if all goes to plan the birds will be flushing in small groups. Depending on the shoot you may hear the command, 'Let the dogs go, let them work it out.' If you have a novice dog do not join in with what quite often becomes a free-for-all; there will be plenty of handlers that let their dogs hunt out the flushing point. Let them do their job and you keep control of your dog.

Cover crops such as maize and canary grass can be the undoing of even the best-controlled gundog. These 'flushing' crops are likely to hold a lot of birds, and this can be very tempting for a young dog.

Another potential danger when you reach the end of a drive, is that quite often your dog will be able to see and hear the Guns and this temptation along with seeing birds falling out of the sky may encourage them to run out through the flushing point and out towards the Guns. You will only want this to happen once. The considerable embarrassment and the earbashing you will inevitably get from the gamekeeper will stay with you for a very long time and that alone is another good reason to make sure your dog is under total control as you reach the end of the drive. There is a train of thought that if you are only ever going to use your dog for beating then do not train or even encourage it to retrieve. That way it will have no instinct to run into the falling birds.

Many ill-informed people may view a beating dog as being the bottom of the food chain as far as dog hierarchy on a shoot day is concerned. It is, however, worth pointing out that in fact they need to be the best-trained dogs on the shoot, and they certainly work the hardest of any of the gundogs. Without their tireless work, there would be fewer birds produced for the Guns to shoot and the gamekeepers' returns would be significantly reduced, yet they are quite often dismissed as 'just a beating dog'. As a beater with a well-trained dog the chances are that you may never get the chance to showcase your dog, unlike a peg dog or a picking-up dog, and at the end of the day you are quite often just grateful that you have managed to get through the day without your dog getting into any trouble. Never underestimate the worth of a good beating dog; they are worth their weight in gold.

A shoot day is a long hard day for a young dog and the chances are that it will be the first opportunity that it will have been working for that length of time. During the day you may well see the dog's reactions start to tail off and it may become less responsive to both whistle and verbal commands. If this happens just get the dog to heel and give it a break. You may even find that it is beneficial just to give a young dog half a day's beating rather than a full day. Remember you will hopefully have nine to ten years' work out of your gundog so there is plenty of time and no need to rush the early experiences.

# 20. Shooting Over Your Dog

When rough shooting, a gundog that will work in the thickest of cover and is steady to the flush and shot is a joy to behold.

When you are walking out to your peg on a driven day you should still have your gundog under proper control, especially if you have your hands full with coats, gun and cartridge bag.

During your gundog's early training you should have trained it to walk to heel both on and off the lead. This lesson should be firmly embedded into the dog's behaviour, and right from the start of the day, especially when walking out to a drive, your dog should be under control and walking at heel right next to you. One of the issues you can come up against when walking out to your peg is that you will be carrying your gun, cartridge bag, maybe a stick and a coat so walking a dog on a lead can be problematic. If you are not confident that your dog will walk properly off the lead due to the excitement of the day, remember during the initial heelwork training the second stage was to wrap the lead loosely around the dog's neck so it thought that it still had a lead on. This can be a good compromise.

Once on your peg you need to decide whether to tether the dog using one of the propriety dog stakes or trust your training and allow him to sit off the lead. You should remember that during a drive it can be very difficult to look for birds flying from the flushing point, aim, shoot, as well as keep an eye on your dog. You really need to be able to multi-task. First things first, if you are going to use a tether make sure it is put in the ground properly. If during a drive your dog does get overly excited the last thing you want is for the tether to pull out and the dog to run off with the lead and stake flying behind it.

Next is the positioning of the dog. Many people will sit the dog right next to them and this is not the ideal place for two reasons. The first is quite simply if you need to reposition your feet to take a shot and the dog is right next to you, it could be all too easy to trip with potentially disastrous results. Secondly, if the dog is sitting next to you, you cannot easily keep watch on it without taking your eyes off the drive. The best place to sit the dog is in front of you with it facing in your direction. That way you can have direct eye contact with it, and it is easier to judge how the dog is coping with the pressure of the day.

Initially, don't let the dog pick up too many birds after the horn has blown. Remember the dog is still young and you need to build up its experience slowly. It also gives you a chance to watch any other dogs that may want to rush in and steal a young dog's retrieve. The most important thing is to ensure you maintain the discipline of a tidy delivery and don't let the dog get sloppy and start to drop birds before you have taken them. One final piece of advice is that before sending your dog out for any retrieves put your gun in the slip and sort out your gear and then you can concentrate on managing the dog. Too many Guns send their dogs out and then carry on picking cartridges up and chatting to the next person in the line and have no idea of what their dogs are up to. That may be fine with an experienced

The best place to sit the dog is in front of you with it facing in your direction.

The best place to sit your gundog when shooting on a driven day is out in front of you so you can keep an eye on it and avoid tripping over as you take your shot.

well-trained dog, but a young dog needs to be watched and controlled at all times.

Rough or walked-up shooting is considered by many to be the poor man's relative of driven game shooting. But in truth there is nothing more exciting and indeed challenging than walking along a hedgerow or overgrown ditch with a gun in your hand whilst watching a dog that you have trained, crashing and bashing the cover in the quest for a wily old cock pheasant or jinking woodcock. To really get the best out of your rough/walked-up shooting dog it needs to have trained to work a good tight quartering pattern and ideally it needs to do this within shotgun range. There is nothing more frustrating than a dog that constantly flushes game out of range especially if game is scarce.

You and your dog will be working as a team and although you will be relying on the dog's highly sensitive nose and hunting drive, you will need to use an element of fieldcraft and shoot straight if you are to be successful. When hunting hedgerows, it is always preferable to work them downwind as this will help to prevent the dog from going through to the other side as it will always prefer to have any scent blowing towards it. Always be ready as you get towards the end of a hedge as quite often the corners are left scrubby and any game that has been pushed down the hedge will be holed up there. In the early days it is better to get someone else to shoot over the dog for you and that way you can keep all your concentration on the dog. If you do have a friend that can help, make sure they understand what you are aiming to achieve with the dog.

Before sending your dog for any retrieves put your gun away and then you can fully concentrate on your dog.

You must keep a high level of concentration and watch your dog closely. A slight increase in pace or tail action can indicate that the dog has winded its quarry. Quite often a dog will feather out on an area in an effort to work out where the scent is coming from especially if it is hunting ground game. The flush when it comes can be an explosive action and you have to

have your wits about you. There have been many heated debates as to whether a rough shooting dog should stop to the flush or run in and make a retrieve as quickly as possible. It is better that the dog stops as soon as any game takes to the wing or runs: that way your shot is not hindered in any way, and you know that your dog is safe.

Once you have taken your shot you can then quickly send the dog to make the retrieve, all under control. More importantly, if you have trained your dog to be steady to both flush and shot it will not go charging off to steal another dog's retrieve. There is nothing worse than having your dog work its socks off to find a pheasant, it gets a nice flush, stops, and gets a good mark on the dead bird only to watch a fellow Gun's dog come charging in and take the retrieve. It is blood-boiling stuff! Another good reason to make sure your dog is steady to birds flushing is that if you are working light cover such as root crops and your dog is out on a retrieve, it can easily bump into a covey of partridges and if it starts chasing the starburst of birds all hell can break loose, and the day's sport can be totally spoilt. Fieldcraft is a skill that is today unfamiliar to many shooting people, but if you are lucky enough to be able to enjoy a few days' rough shooting then it is a skill that will almost certainly add a few more birds in the bag. It is worth learning beforehand as much as you can about your quarry, so you are aware of the kind of cover or areas that they are likely to be hiding.

Rough shooting over a dog that you have trained has to be the ultimate in shooting sports: a true partnership.

Another question that quite often causes debate is whether a rough/walked-up shooting dog needs to be trained to take hand signals. This skill can be very useful especially if the dog has been unsighted when the bird was shot, as can quite often happen when hunting in cover. Ideally the dog should at least be able to take a 'go back' command so you can get it out in the general area, bearing in mind most walked-up birds are shot out in front of the Gun. You could, of course, always walk out to the fall area and work your dog but if you are shooting in a line, you are then walking over areas that may still hold game and this may well be disturbed.

To avoid your gundog running into your barrels when rough shooting, turn your gun around when taking a retrieve.

Take your time when starting the dog off hunting because you are basically going to put all the components of your training into one. You need to give the young dog time to get into its hunting pattern and not be pushed along by you walking too fast. If you get a flush, watch the dog to make sure it stops. If the dog runs in try not to shoot the bird as if the dog gets the retrieve, it has basically rewarded itself and it is no good you reprimanding it once it comes back to you with the bird. If the dog does run in, the best thing you can do is to put the gun away and go back to your training ground and reinforce the dog's steadiness. Like cooking a good meal all the skill is in the preparation and if you really want your gundog to excel as a rough shooting or walked-up companion then be serious about the dog's training and make sure the basics are in place before taking it out into the shooting field.

When the dog returns with the retrieve, turn your gun around so the stock is facing the dog and the barrels are facing away, this will avoid an enthusiastic dog running into the gun and potentially injuring itself. You will be doing a lot of walking when rough shooting over your gundog and if you are lucky enough you may have a few pheasants or rabbits to take home and you will need some means of carrying them. A game or training vest is a far better option than a traditional game bag for carrying not only dummies, but also game. There are two main advantages. The first is that when bending down to take a retrieve from your gundog a game bag can slip round and catch the dog on the head, and this can lead to the dog being reluctant to come right into to the handler. The second advantage is that the design helps to spread the load and makes it far more comfortable when walking long distances.

A training vest is the best way to carry any game that you are lucky enough to shoot.

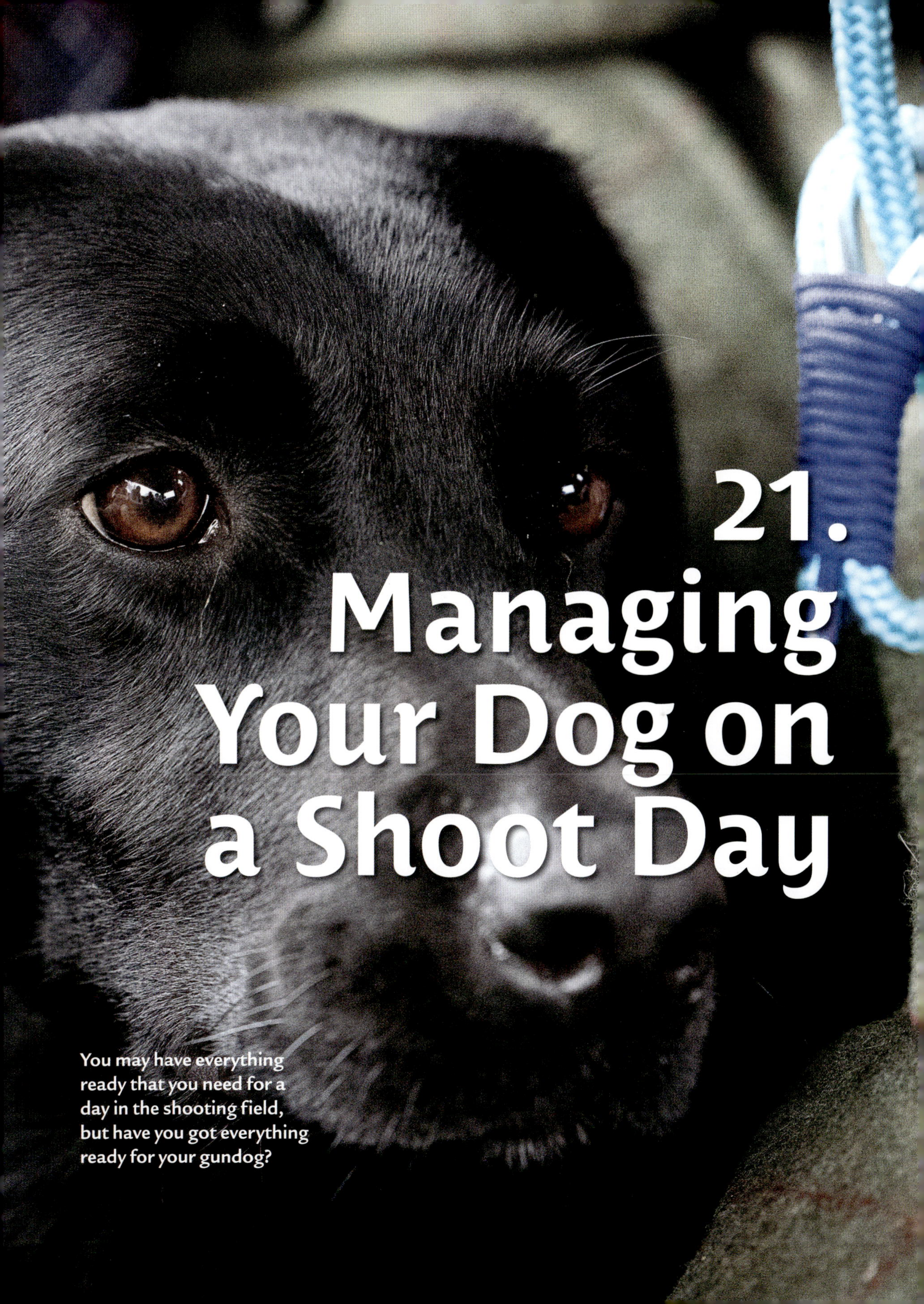

# 21. Managing Your Dog on a Shoot Day

**You may have everything ready that you need for a day in the shooting field, but have you got everything ready for your gundog?**

Our gundogs work hard in all weathers, so make sure they are well looked after at the end of a day's shooting.

The evening before a shoot most of us will be making sure that we have everything packed and ready for the big day. Guns will have been cleaned; cartridge bags will be full to the brim; coats, hats, and boots will all be placed ready next to the back door; but you should also be thinking about what you need to pack so that your dog has everything it needs for the day ahead. It is easy to forget that gundogs are canine athletes, and they need to be looked after properly during a shoot day to ensure they perform at the highest level. There is a debate as to whether a dog should be fed on the morning of a shoot. Ideally they should be given something to eat but perhaps not their full ration. More importantly it should be understood that dogs function based on their reserves, so on the day, having an overfull stomach before working is not a good plan. When you feed your dog before it starts work it will get a rise in blood glucose and this will support exercise, but only in the very short term and it may lead to hindering the use of the dog's energy reserves. A small meal, no more than one-third of the dog's daily diet a couple of hours before you start the day and then feed the balance as soon as you can after you finish, once the dog has cooled down is the best.

Just like humans, during a strenuous hunt the dog's reserves will diminish especially if the weather is cold and wet and so giving a small high-energy snack at lunchtime is a really effective way of topping up their energy levels without overfilling their stomachs. There are plenty of options available from specialist dog feed companies and, although you have a gundog, it is well worth looking at some of the products that are used by the husky or CaniCross racing handlers. These dogs work at a high-energy rate and are required to sustain a high level of work, exactly how you expect your gundog to perform in the field. A note of caution: it has been known for handlers to give their dogs chocolate to boost their energy but be aware that chocolate can be fatal to canines. Just 14 grams per half a kilo of bodyweight may put dogs at risk of chocolate poisoning.

Taking periodic breaks during a day's shooting will help the dogs to relax their muscles and give them some respite to recover, ready to

**Just like humans, during a strenuous hunt the dog's reserves will diminish especially if the weather is cold and wet ...**

start again. Most dogs will let you know when they have had enough, and it is important to recognise these signs or risk injury. A half-hour break is sometimes enough to be able to boost a dog's energy ready to go again. If it is possible, it is a good idea to work the dog, especially the hunting breeds such as spaniels or HPRs, for short periods and then walk them to heel for a bit. This helps to keep them sharp and keen.

Watch out for signs of dehydration in your gundog, especially early in the season when the weather can be quite warm.

The biggest thing to watch out for is dehydration, especially when working the dogs in the autumn when the weather can be still quite warm. Dehydration in dogs occurs when the body loses more fluid than it's taking in. It is normal for a dog's body to gain and lose water throughout the day. Panting, breathing, urinating, defecating,

and evaporation through the paws are all ways your dog will become dehydrated. Dogs do not sweat in the same way as humans and all of the above contribute to normal water loss, which your dog compensates for by eating and drinking. There are signs to look out for and it is well worth being aware of them: loss of skin elasticity, loss of appetite, reduced energy levels and lethargy, panting, sunken, dry-looking eyes, dry nose, dry, sticky gums.

If you suspect your dog is dehydrated, first make sure it drinks fresh, cool water, but do not let them drink too much in one go as this can make them vomit, which will dehydrate them even more. Also try to prevent your dog drinking from puddles as they may contain run-off chemicals from the surrounding fields. There are a number of

Try to avoid your gundog drinking out of puddles as they may contain chemical run-off from the surrounding fields.

Look after your gundog and with luck it will be your shooting companion for ten years or more.

rehydrating solutions available and it is a good idea to carry a bottle or two just in case. Many of these will be more palatable to the dog and therefore encourage them to drink. The best way to protect your dog from dehydration is to make sure it doesn't get in that condition in the first place. Depending on the weather and temperature and the activity level of your dog, it will need more water on some days than others.

If you are fortunate, your gundog will be a constant shooting companion for maybe ten years or more and as they get older their joints will start to show the strain of years of hard work. The one thing you can do to ensure that they do not suffer from the early onset of arthritis or joint problems is to make sure you have a good post-shoot-day regime. Simply by virtue of the time of the year you are out shooting, your dog will get wet and as a result when it finishes working,

the dog can quickly get cold, especially if it is one of the breeds with a finer coat.

Always dry off your dog using microfibre towels, then check all their paws for thorns, stones, and cuts. Run your hands all over their bodies taking particular care to check under their legs. If you have a lot of barbed wire on your shoot, always check right underneath as it is not unusual to find a tear right under the armpit of the dog's leg. This type of injury can go unnoticed and may well get infected if you don't have a regular post-shooting regime. Once the dog has been dried off and checked over, put a towelling drying coat on it. The best ones to use are those that cover all their body and underside. This not only draws the remaining dampness out from their fur, but it also keeps them nice and warm and by the time you get home they are completely dry.

You will invest a lot of time and effort into training your gundog and, all things being equal, they will give you many years of faithful companionship. You owe it to them that you do your best to look after them during your forays into the countryside in pursuit of your chosen quarry.

At the end of the day, check your dog for cuts and thorns, dry them off and use a good quality drying coat.

TARNCRAG
GUNDOGS

# 22. Gundog Terminology

Like all hobbies the gundog world does have a number of commands and phrases that are peculiar to the discipline. In fact, in one way it can be even more confusing as in some cases we use different words or commands for the different breeds of gundogs. Not all of these are relevant in terms of practical gundog training, but it is worth being aware of the terminology.

**Action and style** This refers to the way a dog works when hunting or retrieving. Particularly used in the spaniel world.

**Back wind** Wind directly coming from behind the handler.

**Blind retrieve** A dummy/bird retrieve which has either fallen or been placed out of sight of the dog.

**Blinking** This is when a dog finds dead game and refuses to retrieve it.

**Cheek wind** Wind direction from left or right of the handler.

**Cold game** Previously shot game such as pheasant, duck, partridge, etc., which is cold-stored or frozen and can be used for 'out of season' retrieving practice.

**Cover** Natural or planted vegetation which serves as both protection and concealment for game.

**Creep/creeping** A term used to describe a gundog that slowly moves forward when told to sit.

**D/DC** Stands for docked and dew clawed.

**Dead** A verbal command given to a dog to release a retrieve.

**Decoy/distraction** Any object that may distract a dog away from what it has been sent to retrieve.

**Drive** A term to describe the speed and style of a gundog, especially when entering thick cover such as bramble.

**Dummy** Made from various materials and in numerous shapes. The standard object for teaching retrieving.

**Eye wipe** The term used when one dog fails to find a retrieve and then another dog is tried and is successful or in the case of a field trial it is found by the judges.

**False pointing** When a dog points but no game is produced.

**Fetch** A verbal command used to send a dog out on a seen retrieve. Commonly used for marked retrieves.

| | |
|---|---|
| **Field trial** | A competitive event at which gundogs compete against one another on live game. There are field trials for retrievers, spaniels, pointers, setters and 'HPR' dogs. They should mirror, as closely as possible, a day's shooting in the field. |
| **First dog down** | A field trial term used to describe when the first dog is sent for a retrieve of an injured bird and fails to find it. |
| **Flush** | The act of finding and flushing (making it fly or run) game that is hiding in cover for the Gun to shoot. |
| **FTAW** | 'Field Trial Award Winner'. A dog that has won an award at a field trial, e.g. Certificate of Merit (COM) or higher but has not actually won the trial. |
| **FTCh** | 'Field Trial Champion'. A dog that has won at least three days' worth of field trial open stakes. |
| **FTW** | 'Field Trial Winner'. A dog that has been placed first in a field trial. |
| **Gallery** | A group of individuals observing a field trial; an audience. |
| **Game** | Any species that can be legally hunted for sport, such as pheasant, partridge, grouse, rabbit or hare. |
| **Game bag** | A bag for carrying retrieved game. |
| **Game sense** | A dog's ability to use its natural senses and ability to find dead or injured game. |
| **Game steward** | Someone who will carry and despatch game for a field trial. |
| **Get in** | A spoken command given to a gundog normally meaning to 'get in' water or cover. |
| **Get on** | As per the command 'go back', a verbal instruction used to indicate to your dog to proceed in a straight line until finding a dummy/bird, or it can be used to start a spaniel hunting. |
| **Get out** | A verbal command given to a gundog when using hand signals to send them either left or right. |
| **Give** | A verbal command used to get a gundog to release the retrieved item held by the dog. |

| | |
|---|---|
| **Go back** | Used to send your dog in a straight line until finding a dummy/bird. Often associated with blind retrieves rather than marked retrieves. |
| **Go back and fetch** | Mainly used by HPR handlers when sending the dog out for a retrieve. |
| **Gun sense** | A dog's ability to have awareness of the swing of a gun and to follow the general direction of the shot. |
| **Gun shy** | A dog that fears loud noises, in particular the sound of gunfire. |
| **Handle** | To be able to direct the dog when at a distance from the handler. |
| **Handler** | A broad term relating to anyone in charge of a gundog. |
| **Hard mouth** | A dog that regularly damages game when retrieving. Considered to be a major fault in gundogs. |
| **Heel** | A command that requires the dog to walk beside its handler (normally on the left-hand side) both on and off lead. |
| **Hi lost** | A verbal command given to a gundog meaning to hunt in a particular area when out on a retrieve. |
| **HPR** | A term used to describe a continental group of gundogs that 'hunt, point and retrieve'. |
| **Hup** | A verbal command to 'sit'. Most commonly used in the spaniel world. |
| **Line (taking a line)** | The route a dog takes to the game or dummy going out, and on return to the handler, especially when on a runner (injured but not dead game). |
| **Long line** | A very long training lead. |
| **Making good the ground** | After the initial flush, finding and producing any birds remaining in the immediate vicinity of the original point. This tends to refer to the pointing breeds. |
| **Marked retrieve** | A retrieve that that has actually been seen by the gundog. |
| **Memory retrieve** | A retrieve that has been placed in view of the dog but a period of time and varying distance has elapsed before the dog is actually sent for the retrieve. |

| | |
|---|---|
| **Over** | A command instructing the dog to jump or get over any obstacle such as a stretch of water, a fence, ditch or fallen tree. |
| **Pace** | The speed at which the dog hunts. |
| **Peg dog** | A dog that sits next to a peg and its handler, the Gun, during a drive and may retrieve shot game on command at the end of the drive. |
| **Pegging** | Catching live uninjured or unshot game. |
| **Pick-up dog/ picker-up/picking up** | A handler and dogs who stand well behind the gun line, and systematically retrieve the dead and injured game, or the act of so doing. |
| **Point/pointing** | A gundog that points at game to indicate to the Gun/ handler where the quarry is, normally the HPR breeds or pointer/setter breeds. |
| **Positive training** | A modern approach to gundog training where a food treat or a clicker is used as a way of showing the dog approval of its actions so that it might do it again. |
| **Pottering** | Refers to a dog that hunts without pace or style or one that lingers on an old scent, leaves it and then comes back to it. |
| **Pricked** | Game that has been shot and potentially injured, but not killed. |
| **Quartering/ quarter** | The methodical side-to-side hunting pattern that a flushing or pointing dog is trained to follow in order to cover the ground efficiently and thoroughly. |
| **Recall** | The act of the handler calling the dog to come back to him. |
| **Retrieve** | The sending of the dog and bringing back to hand either a dummy or game: the complete act. |
| **Run in field** | A field trial or working test. This describes the activities that occur whilst a competitor is under the control of the judge. |
| **Run off** | An additional test or run at a field trial or working test. This is used when a judge or judges have been unable to separate two, or sometimes more, dogs for a first place or an award. |

| | |
|---|---|
| **Runner** | A shot and injured bird or ground game that leaves a scent trail along the ground and requires 'picking up' immediately by a dog so that it can be humanely dispatched. |
| **Running in** | When a dog leaves a handler without being sent to retrieve a dummy/bird. |
| **Slip lead** | A lead used by gundog handlers. A slip lead is a combination of both a dog lead and a dog collar, normally made of hemp or nylon. |
| **Soft mouth** | A dog that will pick up and hold game softly but firmly on the retrieve. |
| **Steadiness** | A required skill of any gundog: it should sit still when a bird, ground game or even a dummy is flushed or thrown or when a gun is fired. |
| **Sticking on point** | Reluctance to flush pointed game. |
| **Style** | The tail and body action of a dog when hunting for dummies or game. |
| **There** | A verbal command given to a gundog meaning to hunt in a particular area when out on a retrieve. |
| **To back** | To honour the point of another dog on sight. This would normally refer to the pointing breeds. |
| **To draw on** | To advance steadily on point towards game. Normally refers to the pointing breeds. |
| **To road in** | To work out a scent from point to production. Normally refers to the pointing breeds. |
| **Tongue/ squeaking** | Refers to a dog makes an excited noise such as barking, whining, or squeaking whilst working. This can often occur on the dog's way out to a retrieve and is considered a fault in gundogs. |
| **Turning back on the wind or back casting** | Turning away from the direction of the wind. |
| **Whistle command** | The common way that gundogs are controlled by the use of a natural or manufactured whistle. |
| **Working test** | A competitive event at which gundogs compete. They are normally held in the spring and summer months and use canvas dummies rather than live game. |

‘Hunting is watching your dog work, and taking it easy, and shooting just enough, walking slow, and enjoying the day…’

Quote from Robert Ruark
*The Old Man and the Boy*

# Acknowledgements


| | |
|---|---|
| **Fullpip Ltd** | Supplier of gundog training equipment including the target dummy<br>www.fullpip.co.uk |
| **RRT Launcher** | Manufacturers of remote dummy launchers<br>www.rrtlauncher.com |
| **Active K9 Designs** | Leads, long lines, lanyards<br>www.activek9designs.co.uk |
| **Bull X** | Manufacturers of remote rabbit lure machines<br>www.bull-x.co.uk |

# Index


## A, B

Ball 31, 32, 35, 45, 46, 48–49, 53, 77, 86–89, 90, 91, 103, 106, 126, 155, 163

Beating 10, 19, 31, 39, 43, 71, 86, 91, 99, 131, 177, 201–206

## C

Cover 11, 45, 47, 57, 59, 66, 71, 80–82, 85, 89, 90–93, 103, 119, 121, 128, 149, 150–152, 163, 166, 188, 193, 203–205, 212, 214, 215, 227, 228

## D

Delivery 19, 22, 25, 31, 34, 37, 39, 43, 50–51, 53, 88, 188, 211

Directions 58, 73, 82, 177–181

Drive 9, 11, 40, 57, 71, 77, 85, 94, 99, 113, 114, 121, 131, 132, 151, 159, 169, 185, 193–196, 201, 205–206, 211, 213, 227, 230

Dummies 32–34, 45, 47, 57, 59, 64–67, 78, 79, 89, 91, 103, 106, 108, 115, 117, 119, 120, 121, 124, 126, 137, 143, 144, 146, 169, 171, 177, 186, 201, 216, 231

Dummy launcher 123–127, 131, 139, 162

## E, F

Flushing 71, 79, 91, 100, 121, 126, 202, 204–206, 211, 214, 228, 230

Focus 11, 15, 23, 32, 37, 40, 59, 101

Fur 86, 88, 90, 91, 115, 127, 128, 143, 144, 162, 163, 223

## G

Game 19, 33, 43, 55, 59, 67, 77, 78, 85, 86, 88, 89, 91, 93, 94, 95, 96, 100, 102, 106, 113, 116, 119–122, 124, 126–128, 132–133, 143–146, 149, 152, 160–165, 169, 171, 179, 193–197, 201, 212–216, 227, 228, 231

Pheasant 31, 47, 77, 85, 93, 121, 143, 149, 171, 212, 214, 227, 228

Rabbit 31, 47, 77, 85, 93–96, 99, 121, 123, 126, 127, 128, 137, 143, 162, 164, 201, 228

Gun 36, 53, 55, 59, 71, 86, 106, 125, 131, 132, 133, 137, 138, 139, 185, 196, 211, 212, 213, 215, 228, 229, 230, 231

Gun sense 137–139, 229

## H, I

Hand signals 100, 101, 179, 214, 228

Handling 66, 143, 179

Heel 37, 63, 71–74, 101, 113, 137, 150, 178, 185, 204, 205, 206, 211, 220, 229

HPR 31, 159, 162, 193, 228, 229, 230

Hunting 9, 15, 31, 43, 47, 63, 66, 77, 79, 85–96, 99, 102, 103, 106, 108, 109, 113, 119, 121, 122, 123, 137, 139, 149, 159, 161, 185, 201, 203, 204, 213, 215, 220

## J

Jumping 89, 154–156, 185

## K, L
Labrador 9, 154, 177, 193

## M, N
Marking 77–82

## O
Obstacles 27, 149–154, 230

## P
Peg dog 10, 71, 206, 230

Picking up 10, 31, 36, 39, 43, 57, 77, 78, 87, 115, 116, 137, 143, 145, 146, 149, 159, 161, 162, 163, 165, 169, 177, 193–197, 206, 230

Place board 19–27, 31–40, 47, 48, 51, 99, 100, 105, 113

Puppy 47, 48, 56, 101, 104

## Q
Quarry 86, 94, 96, 113, 127, 161,193, 213, 214, 223, 230

Quartering 86, 106, 121, 139, 161, 212, 230

## R
Rabbit pen 93, 94, 121, 123, 127, 201

Retrieving 9, 20, 31, 43–67, 71, 73, 89, 107, 114, 131, 132, 133, 172, 177, 178, 180, 195, 227, 229

Blind 47, 55, 59, 61, 63, 139, 151, 227

Memory 53, 55, 56, 57, 59, 61, 132, 150, 151, 154, 178, 229

Seen 47, 55, 58, 63, 108, 118, 128, 163, 227

Rough shooting 131, 214, 215

Runner 36, 91, 113, 159–161, 163, 164, 229, 231

Running in 100, 120, 124, 231

## S
Scent 47, 77, 78, 82, 85, 86, 87, 89, 91, 93, 94, 95, 96, 126, 159–165, 187, 204, 213, 230, 231

Scent line 77, 126, 161–165

Shoot day 82, 99, 113, 195, 201, 206, 219–223

Shooting 9, 10, 11, 23, 31, 33, 35, 36, 39, 43, 47, 51, 52, 53, 55, 57, 59, 60, 63, 66, 67, 71, 73, 77, 81, 91, 92, 100, 106, 116, 119, 121, 128, 131, 139, 137, 139, 149, 156, 161, 165, 166, 177, 180, 185, 188, 193, 194, 201, 212, 214, 215, 219, 222, 223, 228

Slip lead 72–73, 169, 231

Spaniel 57, 63, 71, 79, 99, 152, 177, 227, 228, 229

Steadiness 31, 32, 33, 36, 48, 63, 93, 113–128, 145, 170, 178, 194, 215, 231

## T
Treats 19, 20, 21, 35, 104

## U, V
Verbal commands 99, 107, 206

## W, X, Y, Z
Water 162, 185–189, 220–222, 228, 230

Whistle 11, 19, 63, 65, 88, 91, 92, 95, 96, 99–109, 116, 118, 119, 120–122, 128, 145, 156, 178, 201, 206, 231

Wind 58, 82, 87, 91, 121, 126, 145, 159, 164, 187, 227, 231

HÄRKILA
HÄRKILA
CATO
OUTDOORS

# About the Authors

**Nick Ridley** has been writing for the field sports press for more than 25 years and is currently the freelance gundog editor for *Sporting Gun*. He has also written for *Shooting Times*, *Shooting Gazette* and *Sporting Shooter* magazines. Nick owns and works five cocker spaniels in the shooting field and under his kennel prefix Pettycord Gundogs he holds weekly one-to-one and group gundog training lessons.

**Fran Ardley** of Tarncrag Gundogs is based in Cumbria. She has more than 16 years' experience training Labradors, springer spaniels and cocker spaniels, has achieved numerous awards at field trials and has made up two field trial champion cocker spaniels. Fran also runs regular one-to-one and group gundog training sessions.